THE SECRETS
OF DISTINCTIVE DRESS

Photo by Marceau

MARY BROOKS PICKEN

The Secrets of Distinctive Dress

HARMONIOUS, BECOMING, AND BEAUTIFUL DRESS—IT'S VALUE AND HOW TO ACHIEVE IT

BY

MARY BROOKS PICKEN

COMPILED AND WRITTEN FOR

THE WOMAN'S INSTITUTE OF DOMESTIC ARTS AND SCIENCES, INC.

SCRANTON, PA.

INTERNATIONAL TEXTBOOK PRESS
SCRANTON, PA

FOREWORD

The search for happiness carries us as individuals into the country, the streets, the parks, the churches, the homes, the theaters, and to books and magazines.

To know happiness we must appreciate beauty, and to appreciate beauty we must develop it within us

A great degree of happiness may be had from a study of dress and its requisites, for, as we study, observe, and apply, our inner selves will awaken to the artistic side of dress, and once awakened will develop to such an extent as to give us understanding and appreciation.

This book comes to you not as a "Beauty Book," but as a study, and my earnest desire is that it will help you to see in dress beauty that you have not been able to find before.

An artist must know the principles of art to enjoy art or to make a success of it, and so must every woman know the principles of dress and enjoy dress to be successfully clothed.

Dress has such tremendous possibilities, such far-reaching effect, such power for individual success, that no woman can afford not to understand these principles as well as the niceties of dress.

This book does not attempt to exploit historic or ultra-fashionable dress, but to give as simply and directly as possible the fundamentals of dress, to give instruction in the whys and wherefores of individually becoming dress, and to help elevate dress and its requisites to the plane where dress will be appreciated and where it will become a happiness to women

I wish to express my deepest appreciation for the valued suggestions and criticisms of the following friends who so kindly lent their aid by reading the manuscript and suggesting improvements in it: Mrs Belle Armstrong Whitney, of the Whitney Fashion Corporation, author of "What to Wear," New York; Miss Sarah Field Splint, Editor, *Today's Housewife;* Mrs. Margaret Bryce, Fashion Editor, *Pictorial Review;* Walter L. Pyle, A. M., M. D., Philadelphia, Pa.; John Emmet O'Brien, M. D., and Leroy Scott, D. D. S., Scranton, Pa ; and the editor, Mr G. L Weinss, for his splendid and untiring assistance.

Mary Brooks Picken

CONTENTS

ILLUSTRATIONS

THE SECRETS OF DISTINCTIVE DRESS

CHAPTER I

YOUR INDIVIDUALITY

YOUR DISTINCTIVE CHARACTERISTICS—KEYNOTE TO DISTINCTIVE DRESS—OVERCOMING DAME FASHION'S UNREASONABLENESS—SELF-ANALYSIS.

Personality is the outward expression of that indefinable quality known as "individuality." Personality we can develop—can really create. How? By making it express in the fullest sense our highest and best aspirations.

Personalities carry great responsibilities, because we expect them to represent us as individuals. We should therefore clothe our personalities with honest thoughts, high ideals, and lofty purposes; and to enable them to forge ahead—to permit us to reach the pinnacles of our aspirations—we should clothe their dwelling places—our bodies—with agreeable and proper raiment, raiment that will not hamper them but stimulate them to guide our pursuits, to make friends and success for us.

Your individual characteristics should dominate you, your ideas, your attitude toward life and toward those with whom you come in contact.

Your clothes help you to express your innermost thoughts, your kindliness, your good feeling toward all about you—one big and worth-while reason for knowing your good and bad points, knowing yourself well enough to bring out the charm you possess, or to create charm if you feel that you lack this invaluable quality.

You should never be satisfied to be a nonentity in intellect, in understanding, or in friendship You should express your personality in these things, and, in doing this, one of the greatest aids is dressing yourself appropriately, becomingly, and with individuality.

Sometimes, women misinterpret the worth whileness of individuality in attire and resort to freakish costuming. We may be grateful for the infrequency of such mistakes, for there are few women—yes, very few—who do not desire to dress in the prettiest and most becoming way possible, and who will not with aid and encouragement persevere until capable of dressing in a distinctive, beautiful way.

It is my desire in this book to give you authentic and definite information that will enable you to distinguish that which is worth while from that which is not, and so help you in making selections of materials, colors, and designs that will give you garments that will harmonize with your individuality and environment.

The experience of designers and creators of wearing apparel has demonstrated that harmonious dress is simply the result of a proper knowledge of color, basic motifs of design, the kind of fabric to employ for a given purpose, and the lines of the human figure. Therefore, instead of being perplexing, harmonious dress —distinctive dress—is simply the result of good judgment used in selecting colors and fabrics and choosing and adapting styles that, in motifs of design, suit the lines of your figure.

To be clothed in garments that in every way bring out your best points and in no way emphasize any of your defects should be your aim. There are comparatively few women who can afford to be extravagantly dressed; yet, no woman, no matter what her station in life may be, can afford to be shabbily dressed.

Next to your ability—and some claim before it—comes your personal appearance.

Your clothes are your visiting cards—your cards of admission, so to speak—and you cannot afford to be tabooed because of being untidy or dressed unbecomingly.

A really well-dressed woman is never conspicuous nor uncomfortable no matter where she may be To be well dressed, however, does not necessarily mean that you must be extravagantly dressed; it does mean, though, that you must understand dress harmony—how to adapt prevailing styles to harmonize with your personality and to conform to it.

KEYNOTE TO DISTINCTIVE DRESS

The keynote to distinctive dress is to *know yourself*—your good points, as well as your shortcomings. Every little part of your personality has a direct bearing on what you may wear to the best advantage.

Your figure controls the lines of your garments; your complexion, and even your temperament, the color; and your occupation or station in life, the fabric. Yet, coupled to all these is the dominant question of fashion.

It is not wise for any woman to let thoughts of fashion sway her entirely; yet, since clothes are a very important factor and they, in turn, are regulated by style tendencies, it would be unwise to overlook style conditions.

Style has the power of adding much to the appearance of a garment if just a little thought is given to it. Thus, to illustrate my point, suppose we consider a dress or a suit that is, say, only a year old. When new, it was considered very smart; yet in only one short year it seems to have lost the charm it had for us—is no longer satisfactory.

Why this change?

The fabric may be almost as good as when the garment was new, the color is practically the same, and it fits just as well as ever. What else then can it be if it is not the change in fashion—our conception of new lines—that makes the costume appear less attractive to us?

None of your outer garments should be regarded as a meaningless covering; rather, they should be considered as a part of you.

Garments have the power of magnifying physical imperfections—to make one look conspicuous, undignified, and even absurd; also, they have the power to emphasize good points and make one feel comfortable and always at ease. Therefore, by close and careful study, you should endeaver to find out what is most beautiful in yourself, and then set about to express this beauty as cautiously, as carefully, and as appropriately as you can.

Garments of harmonious colorings that are carefully constructed will always tend to enhance one's appearance, and an appropriate costume correctly designed will lend grace to the figure and an ease that aids in the bringing out of one's individuality.

Whatever your station in life may be, therefore, it is really your duty to study the lines of your face and your figure. Then you should give every detail, from the arrangement of your hair to the condition of your shoes, intelligent thought and careful attention. By heeding such advice you will be enabled to select styles that are practical and appropriate and yet becoming.

OVERCOMING DAME FASHION'S UNREASONABLENESS

To emphasize the necessity for a wise selection of wearing apparel, I cannot refrain from mentioning that many women seem to be powerless to overcome the unreasonableness of Dame Fashion.

Every season brings forth new colors and new lines; and many women in their endeavor to be, as they think, fashionable, hasten to adopt these new colorings and new lines without giving any thought as to whether or not they suit their particular type.

To be fashionable does not mean that you should adopt every new fad just as it is given out; rather, it means that you should intelligently readjust the prevailing style so that it will conform to the lines of your face and your figure.

After you give due consideration to dress that is becoming, in no case can you afford to overlook its appropriateness The proper dress, you will find, is the one that agrees with your station in life and with the work that is to be done in it or the purpose for which it is intended. Successful business women, society women, and home women appreciate the necessity of wearing appropriate, becoming costumes in order to be able to cope with all duties that confront them

Besides style and coloring, therefore, the fabric of your garments must receive consideration. The fabrics you select for your dress should invariably be those best suited to your needs, as well as to the season of the year, the time of day in which the garment is to be worn, and the character of the garment.

A knowledge of the things that lead to harmonious dress is valuable to every one It aids in the proper selection of dress, serves to give new courage, new interest, and oftentimes new hope to those who realize its possibilities, and arouses in every woman a love for all that is beautiful, right, and elevating.

All who strive to follow the details that bring about dress harmony will be well repaid, for they will experience the satisfaction of having serviceable, graceful garments that will be healthful, comfortable, stylish, splendid on occasions, and, best of all, garments that will add to their charms rather than detract from them.

SELF-ANALYSIS

Analyze the efforts that have been made to produce a standardized dress for woman, and you will find that there is a legitimate reason for this agitation. Certain women who have become more or less efficient in their dress, and who do not look to the individual becomingness of dress so much as to its service, are trying to persuade women to be more efficient in buying and wearing their clothes.

The dominant question in many minds is, "Will standardized dress make women efficient with regard to dress?" My opinion is to the contrary. I do believe that *individual dress* will bring about efficiency—yes, more than efficiency—because it will give us beautifully and correctly dressed women, a combination very much to be desired.

The woman who is at home all morning and probably goes shopping once or twice a week or to some charity meeting or church gathering and the woman who goes to business every morning do not have the same clothes requirements. The woman who has a limousine to take her about does not have the same clothes requirements as the woman who must walk. The woman who goes to elaborate dinner parties and other evening affairs does not have the same clothes requirements as the woman who has a simple dinner at home with her family The woman who plays golf or tennis and drives her own car does not have the same clothes requirements as the woman who has neither the time nor the inclination to engage in such sports or pleasures.

It would be difficult to put down all types of women and their various clothes requirements, but I hope I have named enough to make clear the necessity for self-analysis. It is for you to decide what kind of clothes you must wear to be becomingly and fittingly dressed. You must realize that if you are going out to business you should not dress as you would if you were going to a church gathering; nor should you, if you are going to an elaborate dinner party, wear a shirtwaist and skirt, as you may be privileged to do at a simple home dinner with your own family or with intimate friends.

It is for you to decide, too, how long a suit or a dress must serve you, whether you must divide your clothes money for a tailored suit, two afternoon dresses, and two evening dresses, or whether you can spend the full amount on a tailored suit and one semi-evening dress that may be used for the afternoon functions that you may attend.

The same analysis should be made in the matter of your hats, shoes, gloves, and all dress accessories, so that you can divide your dress allowance according to your individual needs, and at the same time be sure that you have adhered strictly to the rule of providing becoming and proper clothes

It is better to have one dress or one suit that is becoming and the best your funds can possibly buy than to have two or three garments that might appear cheap and shabby.

To my mind, an old garment of good material that is becoming is much better than a new garment that looks cheap. Do not discard clothes of beautiful materials and good workmanship that are right for you simply because you feel that they are not up to the fashion of the moment. It is better not to procure garments so extreme that they will go out of fashion before the required service is had from them Buy good materials, make them up as appropriately and as attractively as you can, and then be a law unto yourself regarding the amount of wear you get out of them

As you read the instructions in this book, have your own needs constantly before you, not the needs of your neighbor. Remember that becoming dress fitting to *your needs* is the kind of dress for *you.* Keep this thought constantly before you, and you are bound to be benefited. You will be able to dress more attractively and to wear clothes that suit your individuality at less cost; besides, clothes will then mean more to you than ever before.

There are other considerations regarding your individual dress. How much time and thought you can afford to give to your clothes? How much time can you spend in putting on and taking off your clothes? Few women consider these points. They see a dress that is pretty; they like it. But they do not consider how long it is going to take them to put it on and take it off, whether they can afford, in the morning, to take the time required to put such a dress on, provided they must go out to business. Then, too, they do not take into consideration whether it is going to give the service that they require of a dress.

A very prominent American woman writes definitely about the length of time that women give to putting on and taking off their clothes. She says that if women are to succeed in business, they must throw off the shackles of dress. They should so systematize their clothes that they can get into and out of them as quickly as a man gets into and out of his. If men in offices are called on to go into the street quickly, they can don a hat and coat and be properly dressed In many instances, if a woman is going to town shopping, it takes her an hour and a half to get ready to go out; and when she returns she must change, requiring from twenty minutes to half an hour to do this.

Such conditions as I have mentioned make me an enthusiastic advocate of every woman making a self-analysis, anticipating her clothes needs, and determining upon the length of time and the amount of money she can afford to spend on her wardrobe. When every woman appreciates what individual dress will mean to her personally, and then puts her appreciation into practice, we will have women more beautifully and distinctively dressed than ever before, and with the certainty that not half the amount of money or time will be spent as when endeavoring to live up to the standard of dress set for her by her neighbor.

CHAPTER II

THE FIRST REQUISITE

PHYSICAL CLEANLINESS—BATHING THE BODY—CARE OF THE FACE—USE OF COSMETICS—CARE OF THE HANDS—CARE OF THE EYES—WASHING, DRYING, AND DRESSING THE HAIR—THE TEETH—CLEANLINESS OF CLOTHING—"THE OVER-SUNDAY GIRL."

You who desire to be benefited by a study of this book must at the outset realize that perfection of womanhood is to be acquired by persistent, correctly directed effort toward a definite goal.

To be attractive is to be pleasing in face and figure, and you owe it to yourself to emphasize to the utmost every good point you possess, be it big or little. Commonplaceness in a woman is almost a crime. No woman is fair to herself who is dowdy or commonplace, for within every woman, by virtue of her womanhood alone, is the possibility of being attractive if not beautiful.

The greatest essential to a woman's charm of appearance is cleanliness—both moral and physical. Here we are going to consider chiefly physical cleanliness

Bright eyes and an elastic step come from sleeping in a room that is well ventilated and from good digestion and clean intestines. Upon arising or fifteen minutes before breakfast, drink at least one-half glassful of water —three times this quantity is not too much. An orange, half a grape fruit, or an apple the first thing for breakfast will save you many a doctor bill. "An apple a day keeps the doctor away," and an eminent American physician is authority for the truth that there is not a "typical American ill that stewed prunes will not cure."

The water will cleanse the stomach and make it ready for food; the fruit will help the digestive organs and prevent constipation, which is the sworn enemy of bright eyes and a clear complexion. Constipation is usually caused by irregular and improper eating, too much starchy food, and insufficient exercise.

BATHING THE BODY

A bath in tepid water every morning upon arising, plenty of soap, vigorous rubbing, thorough rinsing and drying, cleanses the body of all old skin and impurities. It also stimulates the circulation and gives bodily exercise that could not be secured in any other way.

Look about at your neighbors—in the homes, the classroom, the office, the club. You can invariably tell the woman who bathes frequently and the one who does not A girl whom I knew was persistent in her desire for cleanliness, the keynote of attractiveness Through necessity she lived in a boarding house where only two tub baths a week were allowed each individual and where her room had no heat in winter; yet she took a sponge bath daily and practiced towel rubbing. She said that she thought she would freeze the first few mornings, but after a little practice she could work so quickly that she soon had her skin stimulated and the little red blood corpuscles dancing; and because of this she was comfortable enough to complete her toilet without feeling the severe coldness of her room. She commenced her day physically and mentally fit, and she radiated the charm of perfect cleanliness.

There are physicians who claim that daily baths take needed vitality from frail or nervous persons, but we have yet to meet a woman who was ever the worse for frequent bathing. Some there are who do not have the conveniences for a tub bath every day, but there is always the sponge bath and a vigorous rub with a bath towel to come to the rescue That, at least, every woman should determine to have, and always clean, fresh garments next to the body. Frequent baths, especially foot-baths, with changes of garments are an absolute necessity if one is to reach the "dignity of perfect cleanliness"

True, when we change underclothing every day, the garments apparently are not soiled. Good. Then they may be more easily laundered. Three practically clean garments can be washed as easily as one soiled one. But, remember, they should be well washed. The old skin that comes off the body and the impurities that come out through the pores of the skin must, for health's sake, be removed from the clothing, as well as from the body.

If ironing is a big item as regards time, strength, or expense, knitted or soft cotton crêpe garments will solve the ironing problem, especially for the busy woman. Such garments when washed may be shaken out and hung up straight to dry, thus making it possible for them to be worn in cases of necessity without ironing.

CARE OF THE FACE—USE OF COSMETICS

"Let the pores breathe at night" is a good precept that is never overlooked by the woman who is particular about the care of her face.

Before retiring, no matter what the time may be (it should be, if possible, not later than eleven o'clock if you must be up by seven), wash the face thoroughly, using a pure toilet soap, soap in which there is no free alkali.

Before washing your face, be careful to wash your hands. Many women do not realize the necessity of washing the hands thoroughly before washing the face. Use warm water, a good nail brush, and generous lather. Clean water must be used for the face.

If the face is very grimy, as from travel or outing, apply cold cream to every part of it and then wipe it with a soft cloth Do not rub the cold cream into the face, for the dust and grime will go with it if you do; rather, cleanse the face as well as possible with the cream before the actual washing is begun

Then, wet the hands, and work up as good a lather as possible from a small amount of soap Massage this lather into the face by pressing gently with the tips of the fingers, being careful not to rub so roughly as to cause noticeable wrinkles. Continue the massage over the entire face and neck.

Rinse the lather off with warm water and then with clean lukewarm water; rinse again as thoroughly as possible, and take extra precaution that not a particle of lather remains on the face or neck.

Now wash the face, neck, and ears thoroughly with clean water, using a fresh, soft face cloth The cloth used at this time will help to cleanse the pores and give the face a healthy, rosy glow.

By massaging the face gently and correctly during the process of washing, the facial muscles will be exercised and strengthened, so that lines and sagginess will be prevented.

Last of all, rinse with cold water—ice water is best—or rub a small piece of ice over the face. Cold rinsing contracts the pores and stimulates the circulation.

Dry the face with a very soft towel, and if the skin has a tendency to become dry or chapped, apply a reliable cream. lotion or massage with cold cream.

The appearance of premature old age can be avoided by correct massage of the muscles and skin tissues, but we do know that there are physicians who claim that wrinkles often come indirectly from constipation, and, as neither you nor I can afford such a handicap as wrinkles, we must exercise and eat properly to avoid or overcome whatever causes them. And, if we do not succeed by the simple, natural methods here suggested, we should call on expert help to correct the trouble for us.

To wash the face during the day, use a face cloth and tepid water; no soap is necessary unless the face is actually grimy. Wet the face cloth and rub the face thoroughly; then dry it with a very soft towel. Such washing will, as a rule, clean the face, for usually there is nothing but oil or perspiration to remove Make it a rule to rinse off the face with cold water, and always rub up when washing or drying.

If the face does not seem to be cleansed after the warm-water rinsing and soft-towel drying, use a standard make of cold cream. Massage the cream into the face well with the tips of the fingers, using "more massage than cream." When done, wipe the face with a soft old cloth or absorbent cotton. A good plan is to keep at hand small pieces of soft old muslin, such as that obtained from the skirt of a wornout nainsook night dress.

Many women, when bathing in the surf during the summer apply a generous coating of cold cream and then a thorough powdering to help protect the skin from sunburn

When traveling, if the face needs cleansing during the day, moisten a bit of cotton with delicately scented toilet water and wipe the face thoroughly. This will freshen and cleanse the face in a nice way, because the toilet water is almost as refreshing as a water wash.

After cleansing the face thoroughly, apply a generous supply of face powder and then brush it off with the back of the hand or with a soft cloth.

If rouge is used (sometimes it may be desirable, but rarely), apply it before the powder is put on, so that the face will look as nearly natural as possible and the powder may help to blend the rouge into the skin

There is a great difference of opinion as to the use of things that give surface prettiness, such a rouge, lip sticks, eyebrow pencils, and "beauty patches."

For theatricals, under artificial light, these are almost invariably essential to emphasize certain facial expressions. However, at the opera, theater, dinner, or dance—in fact, at any place where one is in close contact with others—one will be more at ease, more natural, and more beautiful if the surface pretties are sparingly used.

Face powder and talcum are necessary requisites to your dressing table, because their use emphasizes cleanliness, freshness, and care of your personal appearance.

Cosmetics of any kind, especially rouge, lip sticks, and powder, if used, should be of excellent quality in order to be safe. And by excellent quality I mean the kinds that are manufactured by reputable firms and indorsed in advertisements by leading magazines.

There is danger in cheap powder because of the metallic substance used for its foundation More expensive powders, those with rice as their base, dust off more easily than do the cheaper grades.

If you feel that the standard brands are too expensive for you, purchase toilet rice flour. It comes in packages, the same as powder, and is usually unscented, but it gives a fresh, clean appearing surface and is not injurious. It costs very little more than the cheap powders. Corn starch is very inexpensive and is clean, harmless, and delightfully refreshing.

There are several colors of face powders: white, flesh, pink, brunette, and tan. A wise use of coloring in powders is essential

The natural color of the Anglo-Saxon is a soft, creamy color, with a noticeable flush on cheeks and lips. It should be understood that the artist in his attempts to produce flesh color uses cream color with pink In a commercial sense, we think of pale pink as a flesh color. This is not true unless the cream tint is added.

If your skin is unusually white, use pink and tan powders, dusting the face first with the tan and then with the pink and applying the pink to any part of the face that needs building up. For instance, if the face is narrow or if the chin recedes a trifle, emphasize these parts by powdering the face with pink all the way from ear to ear or using it generously on the chin.

Tan or brunette powder is also better to use when the face has been sunburned, as it softens the appearance of the skin, removes any evidence of shininess, and does not emphasize the sunburn so much as white powder.

For the face that appears flushed, white powder is best, with an addition of pink powder to the cheeks, the tip of the chin, and the temples.

For the brunette with a creamy complexion, flesh-colored powder is preferred.

If the nose is prominent, tan powder, with white, rather than flesh, will help to make it less conspicuous.

A judicious and intelligent use of powder will prove of inestimable aid to you if you seriously desire to look your best at all times. Always carry a powder puff or a chamois, a plain and inconspicuous one, and one that is, above all else, clean. A chamois dusted lightly with powder and used frequently and generously, privately, of course, during the day in your home, while calling, or in your office, gives a clean freshness to the face that can be secured in no other way.

If a powder puff or a chamois is not convenient, clean bits of cotton dipped in powder are extremely satisfactory. But they are more expensive both as regards powder and cotton than a chamois, as the chamois, provided it is a good one and is sufficiently large, can be washed frequently and kept in good condition.

A lip stick is a stick of wax colored red, usually by harmless vegetable coloring. It is from one to three inches in length and is used to give color to the lips. Pale lips, which might appear lifeless at a brilliant party where a bright costume is worn, may be given a deeper color by the careful use of a lip stick.

Lip sticks, with many hundreds of women, are in as common use as chamois and powder, though we all must admit they are not so necessary. A lip stick can rarely be used without being definitely evident, and some persons contend that its use will thicken the flesh of the lips—not at all a desirable thing However, every woman should decide for herself whether she can afford, from an ethical point of view, to add color to her lips and whether it really improves her appearance.

If your face has eruptions, consult your physician Digestive or intestinal trouble generally causes them, especially constipation.

Blackheads usually accompany large pores and are very unsightly. One cause for blackheads is that the pores open when the face is washed with warm water, and unless they are thoroughly contracted by the use of cold water or ice they may remain open; then, when powder is put on, it becomes oily and causes a slight infection in the pores.

If you have been annoyed with blackheads for any length of time, it will require patience and persistence to overcome them Frequent bathing, washing the face carefully as directed, and using a piece of ice on the face, especially on the parts affected, will soon conquer these little enemies of facial beauty. It is wise, however, to avoid the unnecessary use of powder while there remains any trace of infected pores. Once the blackheads are removed and systematic bathing is indulged in, powder may be used without annoying results.

If you have growth of superfluous hair on the face, see a competent electric-needle specialist, a medical dermatologist, or your own family physician. Hair can be removed from the face without any injurious after effects, but the work should be done by an expert

If you cannot have this done at once, a small tweezers will give temporary relief, as wild hairs, such as sometimes make their appearance on the chin or grow from moles, may be removed with them.

In pulling hair out with tweezers, put the points of the tweezers up close to the flesh, so that the hair may be pulled out by the root, not merely broken off. If this plan is followed, the hair will require persistent watching, because it grows in quickly. Usually it must be pulled out at least three times a week. Constant pulling out of hair from the face is not recommended, for an electric needle in competent hands will give more permanent and satisfactory results.

CARE OF THE HANDS

Your hands may be such hands as "speak more eloquently than words," and as they do so much for you they deserve more than passing consideration

If it is necessary for you to have your hands in water very much, rinse them thoroughly and dry them carefully. This is better than trying to correct chapped hands resulting from lack of rinsing and drying

If your hands are inclined to chap, apply each night before retiring, after the hands have been made thoroughly clean, a lotion of rose water and glycerine or any other lotion you know to be reliable and agreeable to your skin.

To have presentable hands, your nails require special attention.

Every woman can train herself to be her own manicurist. She need not supply herself with an elaborate outfit, for manicuring can be done just as effectively and at less cost with just the necessary implements

The articles that can be used to advantage in transforming the roughest, ugliest-shaped nails into shiny, transparent, almond-shaped ones are a file, a buffer, sharp curved scissors, an orangewood stick, a cuticle knife, emery boards, a nail brush, cuticle acid, nail polish, and white vaseline.

To prepare for manicuring the nails, hold the fingers for a few minutes in warm soapy water, so as to soften the nails and the cuticle. Then dry the hands, carefully pushing back the cuticle in the drying

Filing the nails on each hand is the next step Give each nail an oval shape, and as nearly as possible have it conform to the shape of the finger tip. Do not hold the file too firmly, and file from the side of the nail toward the center.

Next, wrap a small piece of cotton around the end of an orangewood stick or a similar implement, dip the stick into the cuticle acid, and push back the cuticle; also, run the stick under the tips of the nails in order to remove any stains

Do not cut the cuticle unless it is absolutely necessary. The more often it is cut, the harder and more callous it becomes. It can be trained to remain in proper condition by regularly pushing it back with the orangewood stick and with a towel when drying the hands.

Should there be hangnails, trim them with the scissors, but be careful not to gouge the flesh Applying vaseline to the nails at night will keep the cuticle soft and avoid the formation of hangnails

Should there be scales on the surface of the nails, remove them with the cuticle knife, but be very careful not to scratch the nails Then smooth up the rough, uneven edges of the nails by using an emery board.

Polishing the nails is the next step. Either the cake or the powder form or the small stick of nail polish can be used for this. Dip the buffer into the powder or rub the cake form over it, if the cake form is used, and then draw it back and forth across the nails, one at a time, employing light, even strokes

After using the buffer, wash the hands, using a moderately stiff brush and a good grade of soap, and dry them thoroughly, using the towel to push back the cuticle.

To finish the operation, rub a little of the nail polish over the palm of one hand and rub the nails over this enamel. Repeat the operation for the other hand

CARE OF THE EYES

The eye is the life-spark of the body—"the window of the soul." A clear conscience, a happy heart, and good digestion go a long way toward making your eyes beautiful

Have you ever realized that, as a rule, artists of dress consider the eyes first in deciding on a color for a gown?

Dress to the eyes. If they are unattractive or lacking in brightness, consider the hair and have the color of your gown in harmony with it.

One can never go far wrong, provided the complexion is at all normal, by following the rule of first eyes, then hair. We are all matched up pretty well; in fact, one rarely sees a misfit of eyes, hair, and complexion. If they seem to be out of tune, usually the costume will be found to be at fault, rather than the coloring of the individual.

The eyes, to be attractive, must be clean They come in contact with impurities in the air just as the face and other parts of the body do.

In certain localities where there is much smoke or dust, a small eyecup and a solution of boracic acid may be used to wash the eyes at night after the face has been washed. The boracic acid cleanses the eyes and avoids infection. Washing the eyes in this way will soothe them if you have been in the outdoor air during a considerable part of the day.

Nature provides us with eyebrows and eyelashes to protect our eyes from dust and foreign substances; also, Nature fittingly makes them a frame for the eyes—a frame that helps to bring out the color of the eyes and yet serves to protect them.

Sometimes, usually in response to a fad of fashion, the eyebrows are shaved to produce a fine, shaped line and then blackened with an eyebrow pencil to affect Japanese eye lines, those of a French doll, or an artist's fancy.

It must be admitted that such tampering with Nature, as it were, is sometimes effective, but rarely is it satisfactory or pleasing On the other hand, light eyebrows, that is, eyebrows so fine and light in color that they do not give the proper background for the eyes, may be improved by the deft use of an eyebrow pencil (one may be purchased very reasonably and it will last indefinitely) Such pencils, which are used to give a fine line, may also be made to provide a graceful shaping to the eyebrow by merely coloring the light hair that Nature has supplied, and if the pencil is cleverly and cautiously used such deception will rarely be detected.

More permanent results, however, may be obtained from vaseline sparingly and gently rubbed into the eyebrows and on the lashes each night before retiring.

Frequently the eyelashes are darkened with the pencil or with a very fine brush that has been dipped into coloring matter, but I cannot recommend such a practice, for if a tiny particle should get into the eye serious trouble might result. Eyes are by far too precious for one to run any possible risk of injuring them.

Many women are possessed of a foolish vanity in regard to wearing glasses, and put off wearing them until their eyes are almost beyond help. Rarely is a woman's appearance improved by glasses, but they are a necessity in many cases, and if needed they should be worn. Advice in this connection should always be sought from an oculist of established reputation.

Frequently the need of corrected lenses is manifested in the semi-closing of the eyelids, with associated wrinkling of the skin in and about the eyelids, in constant compensatory pressure on the defective eyeballs. Such chronic facial contortions are a sad substitute for the wearing of proper correcting lenses, with the eyes wide open and the face in repose and unwrinkled.

Eyes that are used for close work should have attention, and glasses are a wise precaution against eye strain and attendant serious results. If they are not provided, severe headaches, squinting, and numerous other ills, as well as unsightly wrinkles, will result, all of which detract from any woman's appearance.

If you must wear glasses, exercise the greatest care to have them correct. If you can afford but one pair of glasses, and it is necessary for you to wear them throughout the day and the evening, have them rimless and fitted with a nose clasp or with bows.

If your nose has a good bridge, eye glasses may be worn successfully, and they are as a rule more becoming than spectacles.

Ordinary spectacles—those with bows—should be resorted to if the bridge of the nose cannot be properly fitted. This holds good if your type of lens or your work demands that the glasses be firmly held in place, or if you have pronounced astigmatism.

Heavy tortoise-shell rimmed glasses are appropriate in an office, for automobiling, or when strictly tailored clothes are worn.

If the eyes are dull and listless, cultivate them Make them sparkle with happiness and glow with kindness. Make them brilliant vouchers of your mentality.

WASHING, DRYING, AND DRESSING THE HAIR

A time-worn and oft-quoted maxim, but one that is nevertheless comforting to many of us, is the pretty truth that "woman's crowning glory is her hair."

Yet most of us abuse our hair unmercifully. We keep it "dressed up" with hairpins, so to speak, while we sleep; we drag the comb through it, regardless of the damage we do; we twist it up in outlandish fashion. Sometimes we permit it to become actually unclean, never stopping to consider that our hair does so much to help us present a good appearance.

The hair should never be neglected, but always well cared for, kept clean, and dressed becomingly.

A mistaken idea exists in many minds relative to washing the hair. There are those who claim that washing the hair injures it. The hair becomes oily, the oil accumulates dust, and the oil and dust clog up the scalp, which is constantly throwing off old skin, the same as the body. Therefore, in order to permit the scalp to live healthily, frequent cleaning is necessary.

Some authorities say that the hair should be washed, under ordinary conditions, once every two weeks. Personally, I have found this plan an agreeable one, as the hair is much prettier after it is thoroughly washed. Some women, because of lack of oil in their hair, find frequent washing undesirable. In such cases, individual experiment and comfort should determine when the hair should be washed.

To prove more conclusively the value of a frequent shampoo, look around you the next time you are with a group of women. Clean, well-groomed hair has life and luster; uncared-for hair, a stringy, dead look. A careful survey will make you eager for the fortnightly shampoo

Many women cannot afford the luxury of having their head shampooed by a professional, nor is this necessary. Many excellent shampoos are on the market, and they may be used with safety in one's own home if directions are followed

To make an inexpensive shampoo, shave off half of a small cake of Ivory soap; over this pour a cupful of water and heat it until the soap is entirely melted. Then beat the soap and water until it becomes a snow-white paste This makes an excellent and absolutely harmless shampoo If there is considerable oil in the hair, or if you cannot wash your hair every two weeks, it may be necessary to add to the paste one-half teaspoonful of soda or a tablespoonful of alcohol to remove surplus oil and make the hair soft and fluffy. Oil of sassafrass or any toilet water gives a delightful scent to the shampoo paste.

The following method of shampooing will be found satisfactory:

Lather the scalp with the paste and rub it thoroughly with the finger tips, so that every part of it will be reached It is not advisable to rub soap on the hair, for sufficient lather remains in the hair after rubbing the scalp to clean it thoroughly.

Rinse out the lather with warm water; then rinse with lukewarm water, then with a little cooler water, and for the last rinsing with water of moderate temperature. These four rinsings are sure to leave the scalp and hair free of soap. The cold water of last rinsing will close the pores and stimulate the scalp.

For gray hair, a very small quantity of toilet ammonia in the water is especially good, as it takes out the yellow caused by the oil and leaves the hair a clear, clean gray. Sometimes a little fleck of ball bluing is put in the last rinse water for gray hair to emphasize further the clean whiteness

To dry the hair, use a clean, soft bath towel. Rub the scalp gently, but thoroughly Press the hair in the towel, so as to absorb as much of the moisture as possible. Then sit near a sunny window or directly in the sun, if possible, and shake the hair gently, but thoroughly, until it is dry. In winter, warm towels are an aid to speedy drying.

When the hair is practically dry, do it up in the way that you know is the most becoming, and arrange a hair net over it, using a net of a color that matches your hair as nearly as possible Do not draw the net tight; rather, have it loose enough to permit the fluffy freshness of the hair to be evident.

By dressing the hair before it becomes "bone dry," a prettier coiffure is possible; also, the hair will be more easily kept in place until the next shampoo.

Well-groomed hair is as attractive as hair of pretty color; a combination of the two is beautiful.

If you have hair of a pretty color, you should by all means dress it attractively, to show that you appreciate your "crowning glory." If your hair is not of an attractive color, keeping it well-groomed and attractively arranged is all the more necessary.

At night, be careful to remove all the hair-pins from your hair and brush and comb it carefully.

Do not use a metal comb Use a good rubber, ivory, celluloid, or bone comb; one that has large, smooth teeth and that may be frequently washed is the best. Also, use a narrow brush with good, firm bristles, because with it you can get nearer the scalp than you can with a wide brush. The hairbrush should be plain and durable, so that it can be washed frequently in good suds, for a brush must be kept absolutely clean.

Separate the hair, brush it gently on each side, and divide it into six strands, three strands on each side. Brush these strands carefully and braid them so as to form one braid on each side of the head. Do not make the braids too tight. Tight braids are injurious; loose braids, helpful.

In the morning, before arranging the hair for the day, brush it thoroughly, so that a neater coiffure will result.

Many women comb the hair up, twist it around, fasten it with a few pins and start out for the day That, of course, is not dressing the hair becomingly; it is merely putting it out of the way.

Study your face and dress your hair to conceal your worst features and to emphasize your best ones.

If your face is round, dress your hair low on the neck or in a high French roll, fluffed in pompadour effect on top and brought gracefully down over the tops of the ears Rarely should you part your hair in the middle.

If you have a large, high forehead, bring your hair gracefully over it, so that your high forehead will not have undue prominence.

The hat and the neck line of the costume have much to do with the dressing of the hair, too. If your neck is thick and short, dress your hair high on your head. If the prettiest spot you possess is the back of your neck, do not conceal it by bringing your hair down or your collar up. Hair dressed low on the neck is more youthful and frequently more becoming, especially to a young, matronly type of woman who is not too fleshy.

If your nose is sharp, do not tell people so by wearing a Psyche knot at the back of your head.

If your face is long and slim, fluff your hair at the sides and make believe that it is not.

If you have pretty ears, do not conceal them by wearing the hair down over the ears. Covering the ears not only narrows the face, but have you ever noticed that frequently those who do this have difficulty with the hearing? Why? Because the air passages are interfered with, and poor hearing results. Air is necessary for the ears, almost as much so as it is necessary for the nose and the mouth And even if this practice were not injurious, why cover up the ear?

The ear of a woman is usually clear pink, not ill-shaped, and there is a note of individuality about it, the attractiveness of which one should emphasize, not conceal.

Remember your ears, then, and remember that the hair should never be severely drawn back, but gracefully brought down not far enough, however, to cover the ear opening

Study the contour of your face. Study pictures of beautiful women. Magazines, especially beauty advertisements in them, contain many pictures of beautiful women. Study these for new ideas of dressing your hair, and when you find a way that you think is just right for you, practice doing your hair like it until you have perfected the style.

Do not try to do your hair all up in one twist. A capable hair dresser will divide the hair into four to eight sections and carefully pin each section in its place until she gets the effect she desires A woman who carefully arranges her hair in the morning, using enough hairpins to give security, will not have a disheveled, careless-appearing head of hair at the end of the day.

And this prompts me to tell you about hairpins. Bone hairpins are softer in the hair than wire ones and should be used in the majority. They should be medium small, and of a color that matches the hair, if possible, so as to be inconspicuous. Small wire hairpins are a necessity and should be used generously to keep all stray locks in place.

Your hair, then, demands careful attention, for it proclaims the well-groomed woman "In cultivating a rose, we care for it, tend, water, and protect it. As a cultivated flower surpasses a weed, so a well-groomed woman surpasses the woman who neglects herself."

THE TEETH

You must keep your teeth absolutely clean, for your good health and attractiveness, too, depend much on them. Use a good tooth brush, one with front bristles longer than those in the body part, and a reliable tooth paste or tooth powder. Brush your teeth thoroughly, using an up-and-down movement and brushing them inside and outside, on the top and on the bottom, so that there will not be a particle of food left on them. Then rinse your mouth thoroughly. Clean them this way at least twice a day—morning and evening Three times a day would be better; in fact, this plan should be practiced whenever possible. Dental floss should also be on hand to clean between the teeth.

Many persons alternate with tooth paste and tooth powder, using one in the morning and the other in the evening. They believe that this is better for the teeth than to use all paste or all powder. The use of a mouth wash will preserve the teeth and freshen the breath, and is frequently advisable.

Visit your dentist every six months; every three months if your teeth are soft

This is by no means an extravagance, but a real economy. Your dentist, if reliable (and you should patronize no other kind), will go over your teeth, clean them, and repair any small cavities. Then, if you observe the necessary precautions in taking care of them, they will serve you three times as long and will reward you by their attractiveness.

Avoid having gold fillings that show A porcelain filling is inconspicuous, and none but a filling of this kind should be permitted in the front of the mouth, except, of course, when gold is the only filling the dentist can use.

Clean, well-preserved teeth, like clean hands and clean hair, have a great bearing on one's personal appearance. They are an evidence of our thorough appreciation of true cleanliness.

CLEANLINESS OF CLOTHING

It seems to me that mention of cleanliness of clothing is not wholly necessary in a work like this, for I truly believe admonition on such a subject is not needed by a woman who appreciates or desires self-improvement enough to seek it

But I cannot let the opportunity pass without emphasizing the need of cleanliness of clothing, for it may encourage you, dear reader, to suggest tactfully, kindly, and wisely the necessity to some one who is lax in this respect

I have been in offices, in classrooms, and even at club assemblages where not merely soiled blouses were worn, but unclean camisoles and brassières.

Once, at a Y. W. C. A. bathing pool, I was shocked to see a vest so unclean that it looked exactly like the color of the cement floor. When the girl who wore it was dressed for the street, she was half presentable; but, though I met her many times afterwards, the vest was the first thing I thought of, and I could never summon the respect I should like to have had for her.

If clothing is scarce, a midweek washing is the solution.

Many girls in shops and offices who appreciate the value of cleanliness wash their blouses, underwear, and hose frequently in order to have a clean supply for the next day. This is a hardship, but one that should be borne faithfully for the sake of cleanliness, which not only gives greater composure and peace of mind, but adds to the comfort of one's coworkers.

An odor of uncleanness among a group of girls or women is offensive, and each person should be scrupulously careful to be so clean that no one will, even for an instant, put her in the class with the offenders.

The use of perfume is in many instances tabooed by women of refinement for the reason that it is used by some careless women to conceal unpleasant odors Cleanness made by soap and clean water and generous rinsing requires no perfume to speak for it.

Delicately scented perfume, toilet waters, and talcum powders, however, are frequently used by discriminating women, never conspicuously, though, merely for the sweetness of perfume and possible sentiment.

Perfumes are so exquisite in their luxuriousness, so refined in their sweetness, as to seem indispensable. They have value, too, in that they are soothing and refreshing. But they have a place—a mission. They are too delicate, too rare, to be abused by misuse, for perfume, you know, is made from the most delicately scented flowers, the choicest blossoms that grow, and should be used as so many drops of condensed beauty.

In some shops, where dark costumes are the required garb, frequently the odor that emanates from a saleswoman is so offensive that much of the joy of shopping is lost.

If dark clothes are the rule, they should be aired at night and kept thoroughly clean, brushed, and pressed.

In many offices, serge or heavy woolen one-piece dresses are desirable for winter wear, and many times only one dress can be afforded. This, however, can be becoming, and it can be kept clean and thoroughly aired.

A dress that must be worn daily should be placed on a chair in front of an open window every night, so that it will be fresh and clean smelling in the morning. At least once a week, it should receive a thorough overhauling and a brush scouring and steam pressing. Frequently, a clean fresh collar of a material in harmony with the dress should be worn, and cuffs, too, if practical.

Sometimes odor is caused by excessive perspiration. This can be overcome easily by the use of harmless perspiration-preventing preparations, which are advertised in reputable publications and sold by reliable druggists. The preventive kind rather than the odor-concealing kind is the more efficacious and is most often preferred.

In cases of excessive perspiration, and there are some, frequently due to nervousness, even the perspiration preventives fail to give absolute protection. In such cases, the use of proper-sized dress shields securely placed in position in garments is not only a protection but a very great economy, for they prolong the wear of a blouse or a waist to a considerable extent Shields, if worn, should be large and of good quality, so that they may be frequently washed with soap and lukewarm water to keep them fresh and clean.

Corsets, too, are a consideration as regards personal cleanliness.

Up to a few years ago, it was thought that the lines of a corset, in fact, almost the corset itself, would vanish with washing, but that thought has been disproved.

A good corset may be washed many times without ill effect The washing should be done with a brush and good suds. Then clean rinse water will complete the task.

A corset will contract, perhaps shrink a little, with the washing, and will make it necessary to have the laces a little looser than before washing; but in a day of wearing—two days at the most—the corset will resume its original size and permit of normal lacing

A book could well be written on the care of the American woman's shoes.

If you would make the best of your shoes, keep them clean and well polished, not merely blackened, if perchance they are black shoes Keep the heels in good repair; this is not an expense, for it saves the shoes. Likewise, keep the laces intact if they are lace shoes, and all the buttons on and buttonholes mended if they are button shoes.

In caring for your shoes, shoe trees are almost necessities. They keep the shoes in shape. If possible, a pair of trees should be provided for every pair of shoes that are in the closet. If shoe trees are not available, it is advisable to stuff the front of the shoes with paper, so that they will retain their shape.

A cretonne shoe box is also an economy and a convenience. A wooden box of a size to accommodate all your shoes, divided into compartments and covered with cretonne and kept in your closet, helps to keep your shoes in place and prevents them from bumping around in the closet and becoming scratched and scarred. If, when you put them in the box, you make sure that they are clean, your shoes will be ready for wear when you want them.

Another reason for thoroughly cleaning your shoes is that dirt and grit cut the leather and cause them to wear out more quickly. Polish possesses advantages in that it keeps dirt and moisture from penetrating the leather.

A prominent and deeply respected business man said that when he was a youngster living on the farm his father found him shining a pair of shoes. "Son, shine the back of your shoes first; then, the front is sure to be shined." I think this is good advice for all, for sometimes the backs of the shoes, especially the heels, are forgotten, and this is almost as bad as no shine at all.

A little shop girl buys a pair of smart, white or light-colored spats or light-topped shoes. They are jaunty and attractive the first few days; then the deplorableness of dirt is evident and they must receive care. If she wears them soiled, she will be branded as careless of her personal grooming If she is to wear them clean, they will require daily care

The woman or girl who wears a soiled pair of white shoes and apologizes for their appearance, using lack of time as her excuse, does not need scolding nearly so much for the soiled shoes as for buying them in the first place. If she cannot find time to keep white shoes clean and cannot afford to have them cleaned, she should never buy them.

As with shoes, so with hose They must be appropriate, as I explain later, and above all clean. Hose should be washed frequently, and the best plan in washing them is to rub them with the hands Hard rubbing on a board wears them out, but frequent changes makes such hard rubbing unnecessary.

"THE OVER-SUNDAY GIRL"

Business men who are interested in their employes, and there are few nowadays who are not, if asked what type of girl makes the greatest success and merits advancement most often, will invariably tell you this: "The girl who takes the week-end holiday for herself and comes to business Monday morning rested, fresh, and clean, her clothes in good repair, a fresh shampoo, and her shoes shined." In fact, this type of girl is appreciated so much that she is frequently called "The Over-Sunday Girl"

We must be clean and presentable. We must be in touch with conditions and have a mind clear and open, a mind scintillating with ideas, if we hope to achieve success.

And, you, as well as every girl or woman, are entitled to a measure of success. It will come if you build your defenses by learning the value of education and good health, the necessity of correct attire, and the far-reaching effects of an attractive personality. Take stock of yourself. Give yourself a fair show by making the most of every attractive point you possess, both of mind and body. Imitate if you will, but only the *best,* and do it well. Proper regard for the "intimate little feminine things"—that is the secret of charming individuality.

Campbell Studios

PEGGY WOOD

Clothes help Peggy Wood to play the part of Sweetheart, Grandmother, and Granddaughter in one play, "Maytime" Virtually this Youth to old age and to youth again in one evening

Photos by White

CHAPTER III

APPROPRIATE DRESS

STATION IN LIFE—OCCASION—SEASON—SHOES AND HOSE—HATS, VEILS, AND GLOVES—THE WEARING OF FURS—THE WEARING OF JEWELRY—THE WEARING OF FLOWERS—DRESSING APPROPRIATELY—CULTIVATING INTELLIGENCE IN DRESS—A CLOTHES TRIUMPH.

Much has been written on the subject of "station in life" In the older countries marked distinction exists between people of wealth and rank and the peasantry.

In France, the peasant women delight in wearing their caps and aprons; in fact, it is almost an unheard-of thing for a peasant woman to be without them, for they take great pride in honest toil and want it known that they are "in service"

In America, there are no such class distinctions. Here daughters from every country are blended in the making of American women; but even in this great Democracy appropriateness of dress should be understood and observed.

If your position in life is such that you are looked up to and respected by your friends and the community at large, you should be careful almost to a point of fastidiousness in the matter of clothes. Regardless of where you live or how many people you meet in the day, there are some who may be affected by your knowledge and appreciation of dress or your lack of it For this reason, if for no other, you should be exceedingly careful to give no one a chance to misjudge or criticize you.

We never know what effect our example will have on our associates. To enjoy peace of mind and do our part well, we should make sure that our conduct and morals are above reproach and our style of dressing beyond criticism. For the woman of moderate means to be well dressed entails no hardships, for dignified economy and good taste invariably go hand in hand.

When we see a young girl or a woman dressed in extravagant fineries and we know that her income or that of her father or her husband is too small to support such a display, we cannot help but pity her and often, unfortunately, question her integrity. No woman should place herself in a position where she will be the object of undeserved sympathy or suspicion.

There are some men who look on womankind as a whole as a bundle of lace and ribbon, and measure their business intelligence by this standard. This is unfair and the pity is that those responsible for it are women who are unable to discriminate where feminine finery is concerned. Nothing is more exquisitely feminine and attractive than fluffy lace and dainty ribbon used in the right place and at the right time, and nothing more unattractive than the display of such finery in inappropriate surroundings.

The love of pretty clothes is the cause of much unhappiness to many girls. Every girl should be taught from earliest childhood the value of the right kinds of clothes, as well as when and where to wear garments of certain types.

If girls are taught early in life the principles of correct dress and the value of strict adherence to the rules of correct dressing, they would not appear at the office in the morning with a hat that is appropriate only for afternoon or evening wear, with thin silk stockings, with chiffon blouses, and an excess of jewelry; rather, they would prize these things enough to keep them for the proper occasion, and, for the office, wear clothes that are comfortable, practical, and appropriate—clothes that will make it possible for them to give a good full day of intelligent service.

Many club women and others interested in civic affairs have discussed the possibility of trying to teach young girls in offices and shops the appropriateness of dress.

Usually, such efforts, after investigation, come to naught, for the reason that these enthusiasts realize that dress is largely an individual problem, one that no corporation or firm can handle, except by making iron-clad rules, which usually result in a uniform.

This, though economical from the individual's point of view, is not desirable nor practical for small offices and institutions Rather, in such places, it is better to display individuality in one's attire with good taste as the distinguishing feature.

A new era in woman's clothes is dawning, or, rather, a new outlook has been acquired by many. In factories and public places where women are employed to do the work of men, they wear bloomers and Russian blouses; or, sometimes, they wear full hip trousers, leggings, and a coat that gives the costume the appearance of a riding habit

Such costumes are appropriate if worn when necessity demands They should be chosen discreetly, however, as a woman's figure differs from that of a man. Such a costume should be full enough over the hips and thighs and correctly fitted over the bust to avoid emphasizing the presence of flesh.

If a woman's work is such as to demand a mannish costume, there is no reason why she should not wear it with comfort and grace and be just as much a gentlewoman as she would be in the most feminine costume A real gentlewoman never needs to tell you that she is a gentlewoman Her presence speaks more convincingly than words.

OCCASION

A great number of magazine articles have dwelt at length upon appropriateness in dress, and especially appropriate dress for all occasions; yet, with all that has been written and said upon this interesting and far-reaching subject, we see on every hand and on all occasions costumes that make the wearers conspicuous because of their inappropriateness.

For example, at an informal gathering of young women, all simply attired—most of them wore their business dresses, as it was a business meeting held in the early evening—one young woman came in a low neck, sleeveless evening gown She was conspicuous, and doubtless was most uncomfortable. Had it not been for the level-headedness of the other young women present, the appearance of this gay butterfly in the midst of these busy young bees might have caused a serious mental disturbance, as the meeting had been called for the discussion of personal development.

Another time, I was disturbed to see a young woman hastening across the street, a market street it was, in sleeved apron and boudoir cap—a fussy, lacy cap that would have been pretty in her bedroom, but words are inadequate to express its "out-of-placeness" on a public thoroughfare

Another example: In a dietetics class held in the forenoon in a classroom, a young woman of good family wore a bedraggled afternoon dress, doubtless with the thought of wearing it out and getting as much good out of it as possible. The dress was distracting to the other members of the class, and the criticism she subjected herself to was costly—more costly than a simple businesslike dress befitting the occasion.

When we learn, as a people, to take the matter of dress seriously and conscientiously, study it as we would the subject of food for the table or reading matter for the development of the intellect, we will have removed ourselves from the pale of criticism and will be appreciated for the common sense and good taste expressed in our attire.

SEASON

One's physical comfort frequently keeps a very good check on appropriate dress for the season. For instance, on a midsummer's day, particularly in the warm climate of the Southern and Central States, it is rare to see a dress of wool, especially of a dark color, except when worn through necessity Not many years ago, however, if a woman had one black woolen dress (or possibly it was silk), it served for church service every Sunday in the year, and was also due to serve for the Fourth-of-July celebration

Elderly mothers have come to realize that they look ten years younger and are ten times more comfortable on a warm summer's day in a pretty, soft white dress, and it is pleasing to see a group of such mothers dressed in pretty, light wash dresses, as they appear many times as attractive as a group of young women.

For summer wear in offices, a low-necked and short-sleeved frock, with inadequate petticoats, no matter how pleasing the color or how pretty the design or how becoming, is not appropriate.

A simple frock of modest design and coloring or white, with a modest neck and reasonably short sleeves and with adequate petticoats

—one with a double front—is entirely appropriate. In fact, such a frock is pleasing and comfortable for business, provided both dress and petticoats are absolutely clean

Milliners, dressmakers, and merchants, to offset the lull after Christmas, begin showing spring suits and spring hats, and it is not uncommon to see in the coldest days of January a straw hat and low shoes, and in the warmest days of July, furs, and frequently heavy hats of velvet and fur. Pages and pages condemning this practice have appeared in trade papers and magazines, but it is becoming so established that sometimes one feels almost conspicuous in a winter hat after the first of February and in a summer hat after the middle of July.

This condition should not exist, because it is illogical and inconsistent. Such practices create business for the milliners and merchants at the expense of women who are martyrs to fashion. The only way this condition can be adjusted is for every woman to be a law unto herself regarding the wearing of out-of-season clothes.

The buying of cheap clothes is false economy. Buy good, conservative clothes, take care of them, and wear them more than one season, if necessary.

When spring comes and the winter coat, hat, and furs are to be put away, brush them, clean them thoroughly, and take care to store them where they will not become unduly wrinkled. When clothes become too wrinkled, it is almost impossible to get them to look presentable again The most careful steaming and pressing will not get them into their original condition.

In hanging clothes away, place them carefully on hangers in clothes sacks in your closet, so that they will be safe from dust and in good condition when you have occasion to wear them. To guard against damage from moths, put moth preventives in the sack.

Before you buy your next winter's outfit, get out these things you have carefully put away and see what repairing and remodeling are necessary to make them wearable.

You will be surprised to find how much better your things will look than you had anticipated, and that frequently many dollars can be saved by making use of some of your last season's clothes

In the winter, it is frequently convenient to wear little summer dresses about the house. However, if your summer dresses are not to be worn during the winter, wash them free of starch and put them away in bags or boxes.

Garments made of white material should be put into a light-colored bag that has been thoroughly blued so that they will not become yellow.

Summer hats are rarely wearable the second season, unless they are of good straw or braid and can be reblocked or redyed. But a hat, be it a summer or a winter one, should be put away with care, because, frequently, there are trimmings that can be utilized in making a new hat or for some other purpose.

SHOES AND HOSE

A neat shoe is a necessity for a tiny foot How distressing it is to see an attractive foot in a shabby or unkempt shoe. And a large foot—well, it must of necessity be well-shod, shod in a way that will not attract attention to it.

When buying shoes, always have your foot measured. Do not try to give your size and insist upon having it, because you may have gained or lost flesh, and this gain or loss is evident on your foot the same as on your hands or any other part of the body. Then, too, shoes manufactured by different firms are made on different lasts, and the same size-number may be larger or smaller, according to the last used.

Shoes should never be tight. Tight shoes cause many ills, and no one can ever appear graceful or at ease in a shoe that is uncomfortable.

It is economical as well as comfortable to have several pairs of shoes, as it rests the foot to wear different shoes. The leather frequently is softer in one pair than in another and consequently the feet are made a little more comfortable by the change.

Much is added to the attractiveness of a costume if proper shoes are worn.

In selecting shoes to wear with certain dresses, exercise care to have the leather of the shoes correspond with the texture of the dress. For instance, soft silk dresses, such as charmeuse and satin, are really better with low fine kid or patent-leather shoes, and, the shoes being low, silk stockings help to soften the lines of the foot.

Patent-leather shoes, oxfords, and slippers are frequently desirable for wear with lingerie dresses, as well as with silk and satin dresses.

If it is not practicable to wear low shoes, cloth-top shoes or very fine kid-top shoes with light soles are in good taste There are times, however, when "cloth tops" cannot be procured, even though they do seem to be more agreeable for soft dresses.

The hard-surface woolen materials, such as heavy cheviots, serges, tweeds, and novelty suitings, seem to call for shoes of reasonably heavy leather, usually dark tan, brown, or black.

The wearing of button or lace shoes is usually controlled by fashion. When lace shoes are in fashion, it is almost impossible to purchase button shoes, and vice versa.

Remember that, in the house, the heavy shoes you have worn on the street are not appropriate, especially if you change to a house dress. Besides, if you establish the habit of changing from street shoes to house shoes while you are in the house, your feet and your shoes will be better for it, and you will enjoy much greater comfort.

We should cultivate a little of the English woman's accuracy in wearing the right thing at the right time.

A tailored suit calls for a shoe with a plain heel, not by any means a French heel. Some women, in their desire to appear appropriately dressed, wear a low-heeled walking shoe with their tailored suits and a French heel with their afternoon and evening gowns. This practice cannot be carried out without serious results, because changing the position of the foot weakens the arches, causes considerable strain, tires the feet, and frequently causes swelling

Physicians disagree about the wearing of high- and low-heeled shoes.

It seems logical that a reasonably low heel gives greater comfort and is more sensible, but the high heels have had the favor of the majority for so long a time that they have come to be a factor that must be reckoned with. High heels are attractive, because they make the foot appear smaller, add a little to the height, and help a woman to stand straighter than she would, perhaps, with low heels

Common sense tells us that the low heels are better; our pride tells us that the high heels look better on us Then why not strike a happy medium and wear a heel that is not too high nor too low?

Heels one and one-half or one and seven-eighths inches high cannot do any injury, and they are usually more attractive than lower heels. The heel height of one's shoes should be uniform, so that the feet will always be in the same position.

A woman's hose should match her shoes in color, and black hose should be worn with black shoes Unless your dress is white or light-colored, do not wear light-colored or white hose with dark shoes.

Sometimes it is advisable to have the foot portion of the hose white. In such cases, buy hose that have white feet. Do not try to wear low shoes with such hose, for the white will almost always show and make your feet appear ordinary.

If your shoes have light tops, wear hose to match them. But do not wear conspicuous hose unless it is with a sports costume. A girl playing tennis and wearing a white dress, a red tie, and red hose makes a pleasing picture. A bathing costume, also, will permit the wearing of hose of a color to match the trimming color on the costume.

A young girl on the street in gaudy hose attracts undue attention and possibly, unthinkingly, unkind criticism. A gentlewoman never attracts attention to her feet or her legs. She takes particular pains to have hose of an inconspicuous color and entirely in keeping with her shoes and costume.

There is a great difference of opinion on the question of silk hose. Many people contend that silk hose should not be worn by a woman or a girl of limited circumstances, because they are a luxury, an extravagance.

Of course it must be admitted that good silk hose cost more than twice as much as lisle. Yet silk hose are not an extravagance if they are carefully washed and kept in good repair If they are of good quality (not as thin as netting) and are properly taken care of, they will last a little longer than cotton and lisle hose; and, besides, they are more comfortable and look ever so much better.

In recommending silk hose, it is not my intention to underrate the value of lisle hose, for they are very comfortable and economical, and many prefer them to silk hose. A woman or a girl who is careless of her clothes, who has a small income, and who cannot properly care for silk hose should not wear them.

Putting the hose on properly has much to do with their wearing possibilities. Try the following method: Gather the top of the hose over your hand until you have almost reached the foot; then slip the foot of the hose over your foot, adjust it properly, and pull up the leg portion. This prevents pulling of the threads, or "runs," which are the bane of all silk-stocking devotees.

Most fastidious women insist upon the seam of the hose being directly in the center of the calf of the leg and absolutely straight. The psychological effect of this care in putting the hose on straight is important in itself, for if we are careful about such little details we will be careful about the more important ones

We talk about clothes making a background for us, of having our dresses made of a color that harmonizes with our individuality, and even of having our coat linings of such a color that when they are thrown back on our chair they add to the background of the picture. But do we realize fully the value of the right hat—the individual hat, the hat that makes a background for our eyes, our face, our hair?

The greatest dress artists say: "Dress to the eyes; if the eyes are not definite enough in color, dress to the hair, not forgetting the contour of the face."

We must expect a great deal from our hats. They must make a frame for the face. The kindliness and good cheer, the spirit of life, that our faces express for us must have a fitting background. If we are not in our homes, then our hats must be intimate enough to make a desirable background.

If plain dresses and plain suits, i. e., tailored frocks and suits, are becoming to you, you will almost invariably find that tailored hats are becoming.

Pretty-faced girls and women with luxuriant hair may wear small hats well. Pretty faces in which no lines have formed and the kindly face of the mother, with lines that mean a very great deal, may also have a small hat as a background. But the "in-between" woman, with lines showing in her face when it does not seem quite time for them, should wear a hat that has enough brim to overshadow the lines.

It has been said that the woman who has lines in her face should try to have hats with dark facings, because a light facing in her hat will allow every line to show and make the face less attractive.

Some women can wear an all-white hat with a white dress, for the reflection coming up from the dress will soften the lines enough to make the white hat agreeable and becoming.

When you are buying a hat, try a number on. Look at them from the front, the back, and the sides, and study their lines and coloring intelligently. Walk about with the hat on Sometimes, when you are sitting, the hat may be very pretty, but when you stand you may find that you are too tall or not tall enough for that shape of hat

Never buy a hat hastily nor without considering whether it is becoming to your face, whether it is suitable for your hair, or whether it is agreeable in color and appropriate for wear with the garments, suits, or dresses that you have. If the hat is to be worn with some particular suit or coat, have that garment on, so that exactly the right effect may be attained. Remember that much of the smartness of your costume depends on your hat. You should give it great consideration and be sure that it is right for you in every particular.

At some time you may have been so disappointed with a certain shape of hat that you continually avoid getting a hat of that kind again Perhaps, though, there was some particular line or color that made it unbecoming; so, when the opportunity presents itself, do not hesitate to try on a hat of a similar shape, because you may find one that is becoming.

Another thing to remember is that if you gain or lose weight you may have to change the shape of your hat. A shape that is desirable for a slender figure is not agreeable for a stout one, and the shape that you wore at twenty may not be becoming when you are thirty or forty.

Beautiful picture hats, especially those of black and dark colors, are wonderful in the right place—at a fashionable restaurant, a hotel dining room, or an afternoon social function—but they are not suitable for business or street wear.

Faded flowers, bedraggled feathers, and crumpled chiffons are not pleasing in hats.

Veils, like perfume, are an exquisite luxury, if they are dainty, delicate, and becoming. Beautiful veils can cover a "multitude of sins," and rarely are they ugly.

Veils sometimes seem out of place; at other times they seem straggly. However, if they are worn for a reason—to enhance the beauty of the hat, to give the appearance of a more complete toilet, to protect the face, all logical reasons—then they are very desirable.

Always wear veils with care and discrimination. They should be of a color and weave that you know will add to your attractiveness, and they should not be so heavy, unless they are for motoring or outing, as to conceal your features.

In purchasing and wearing veils, follow fashion dictations as far as is logical, for frequently very smart effects may be produced by the addition of a veil.

Gloves, romantic, yet necessary articles of wear, like dainty handkerchiefs, bespeak the nicest niceties of the wearer. Gloves should be in accord with the costume always, and—always clean and carefully fitted. Fine kid gloves are delightful possessions, but they are more extravagant than washable kid, lisle, or silk. Kid gloves with furs, silk gloves with lingerie dresses, is a rule that can be followed out with surety.

THE WEARING OF FURS

Character seems to be expressed to a very great extent in furs. We all seem to know the woman who wears beaver, mole, skunk, fox, mink, sable, and ermine. Every woman has her preference as to fur, and you can usually wear the fur that you like best, provided you combine it with suitable material or arrange the shaping so that it is becoming to you.

An aristocratic young woman, slender and graceful, with hair that is beautifully dressed and a gown that has attractive coloring, may, if her pocketbook permits, wear ermine.

Women from thirty to fifty can wear scarfs of mole to splendid advantage, especially if it is combined with the darkest American-Beauty shades or with a color or a material that will give life to supplant the lack of color in the mole skin.

Skunk, red fox, and any of the long-haired furs should not be worn by any person who is not absolutely tidy in every particular. Straggly hair, irregular skirt and coat lengths, and a draggly get-up do not combine well with long-haired furs. In such a case, a short-haired, compact fur piece will be more attractive, because it will help to give neatness rather than emphasize the lack of it

Some dress artists say that heads on furs are extremely poor taste and should never be worn This is largely a matter of individual taste. Personally, I should not enjoy the heads, because there is a soft familiarity of furs that I like and which, I fear, the animal heads might take away.

Furs are beautiful, and if you wear them in the right place with the right effect, they will actually *make* a costume. But when you wear them just because you possess them, without regard to place or costume, you err against one of the fine principles of dress and openly insult one of the most beautiful of our dress accessories

If you possess furs that were not selected especially for your requirements and in accord with your individuality, do not consider them hopeless. If they are good furs, go to a dependable furrier and try on furs from his stock until you find a shape and size that is becoming Then, see what you can do about altering your furs to assume a similar shaping. Satin of excellent quality and of a color that is suitable can very frequently be combined with fur in a delightful way.

If your furs are more valuable, and possibly more becoming, than you feel your suit will be, plan your suit to bring out the beauty of the furs.

Furs should enrich costume, never detract from it. They should give evidence of "luxurious warmth"—a very good reason why you should not wear them on July Fourth or on an August day, unless, of course, you are in a climate where the warmth of a soft beautiful fur gives comfort in midsummer.

THE WEARING OF JEWELRY

Usually, jewelry is given to us; rarely is it purchased for our particular requirements. Somebody wants to give us something very pretty and gives us jewelry that appeals to him or to her, seldom taking into consideration whether it harmonizes with our individuality or not.

This is a pity, because jewelry is one thing that seems convenient to give to those we care a great deal for. If we must give jewelry, we must use great care in selecting it, so that the person who is to receive it can wear it comfortably and feel that it is appropriate.

A dear mother whom I know possesses a pair of earrings and a lavaliere that would be pretty on a girl of eighteen or twenty, but they detract so much from her dignity that, to be a real friend, you would feel that you should tell her of their inappropriateness for her But she treasures them dearly, because they are gifts of two sons that she loves very much It is evident that she has never considered whether or not she should wear them, but has worn them almost continually because her loved ones gave them to her.

I appreciate sentiment so much that I should hesitate to tell this mother that she should not wear these pieces of jewelry, but in conformity with the rules of appropriate dress one has to say definitely that she should not.

It is said that only brilliant women—that is, intelligent women who are beautifully gowned and handsome both as to face and figure—should wear diamonds, because their very being should sparkle in company with the beautiful stones; yet the joy that one feels in the possession of even one beautiful stone seems like a sufficient excuse to warrant the wearing of diamonds by every person who can afford them.

But, again, if we are to practice the correct rules of dress and apply them persistently to ourselves, we must persist in sacrifice, and sometimes this means sacrificing the very things we like best. To be beautiful, attractive, and appropriately dressed is a serious undertaking, but you can be all this if you make persistency your watchword.

Many ultrarich women own exquisite jewels, and frequently they wear them because they possess them, and not because the jewels are appropriate. On the other hand, many do wear jewels with due regard to their place and decorative value.

A string of pearls can enhance a soft, lacy costume and add a great deal to its attractiveness and individual becomingness Pearls can be worn, too, with exquisite soft velvets and satins, but they require a fitting background to make them most beautiful.

I once knew a woman who wore topazes in simple plain settings with her brown costumes. She had brown hair and brown eyes, and the topazes added just enough life to her costumes to make them decidedly fetching. Another woman I knew wore corals with soft gray and another wore amethysts with pink-tans and pink-grays, all of which added to their attractiveness. The dresses with which these jewels were worn were simple in design and not overtrimmed, thus giving the jewels decorative value—a chance to brighten the costumes and to express individuality in a delightful way.

A graceful string of jet black beads frequently adds just the right touch to a costume that seems a flat mass of color and needs something to add smartness to it. Corals and pearl beads also may be used for the same purpose, but they should be used with a color that they either subdue or brighten.

I want you to understand my meaning here For instance, a turquoise evening gown of satin that seems a mass of brilliant color may be subdued by the addition of a string of black beads that give line to the gown and help to quiet the color. On the other hand, black jet beads worn with a lusterless black gown will brighten it.

A brooch should not be worn for mere adornment It should have a purpose and be used at the termination of the neck line or to hold some part of the costume in place. It should not be placed on the gown merely because you possess it and desire to wear it.

I recall a sewing class in which we openly discussed correct and incorrect dress. After having weekly meetings for a year, I felt that the entire membership was well informed as to correct and incorrect dress, and I was proud to meet any member, because each expressed the little niceties of dress we had tried to instill and cultivate.

One woman, I remember quite distinctly, seemed deeply impressed with what had been said about jewels, and, with means at her command, insisted on wearing jewelry that harmonized with her costumes. She took particular pains to harmonize them in color, because she seemed to have this point definitely in mind, but she entirely lost sight of the shape and appropriateness of the jewelry.

She was a frail creature with little color, and we had decided by experiment that deep red (burgundy) was the most appropriate color for her She had seen a demonstration of a brown-and-topaz combination and was thrilled by the beauty of it, so she proceeded to buy a very dark-red velvet dress, deep and rich in color and beautiful in texture. Then she purchased a garnet necklace arranged in a heavy gold mounting, the gold taking away the beauty of the red velvet and making the garnet so hard and unfriendly that it seemed to be an absolute stranger to her—a thing we should never permit in anything that we wear.

Our clothes—every stitch, even our handkerchiefs—should express our individuality, express us in the most beautiful way possible.

The necklace that I have mentioned cost considerable money, and it took courage to say to my friend:

"Don't you think the pearls you have would be better for wear with your velvet gown? I am sure I should like them better, because they would be 'more friendly' to you. They would give the softness and whiteness at the neck that your gown needs"

Always remember that the jewelry you wear must be worn with consideration, not to make you appear as if you were advertising a cheap jewelry establishment.

Always ask yourself: Does the piece of jewelry add to the appearance of my gown? Does it seem to have a place there? Would a person in looking at me see my gown first and then find the jewels there as a part of the gown, or would the jewels stand out as being merely adornment and not a part of the color scheme or line effect that I wish my gown to express for me?

I have always been a believer in wearing good things, feeling that cheap clothes, cheap jewels, cheap anything, express cheapness of person and "cheapness of mentality"; and rather than have cheap jewels, I would not have any. But I have frequently had gowns where a little inexpensive brooch, or sometimes a string of beads, was just the right color, size, and shape to add to the beauty of the gown and make it seem more complete

There are many shops that sell inexpensive things that are exquisite in workmanship. Frequently, copies of beautiful pieces of jewelry that can be worn during the life of a gown can be bought for a reasonable sum, and then they can be laid aside for some future time without a feeling of loss.

Of course, if a woman knows that brown, gray, purple, white, or black is her particular color and she always wears such colors in the majority, she frequently can afford to purchase jewels that are rare in quality and beautiful in design, because she will need so few when she holds definitely to one color scheme and similar style.

Another precaution about wearing jewelry: Do not wear all the jewelry you possess at one time.

Do not wear silver and gold together, unless they are combined to form a design

If the sleeves of your gown are short, and you feel that a bracelet will break the length of the arm or make it more attractive, no doubt it will be just the right thing. If it does not really show pleasing improvement, do not wear it.

In wearing rings, make sure that they are in accord with the garments you wear and try to avoid burdening your fingers with them.

Earrings, too, merit consideration. Sometimes they enhance a costume, emphasize a completeness of toilet that is pleasing; at other times they are so out of place as to appear almost barbaric.

It is not uncommon to see a young woman wearing all at one time a watch pinned to her blouse, several rings, from one to three bracelets, and a string of beads. Such a sight tells you that she is not practicing the rule of elimination or applying the laws of harmonious dress to herself.

THE WEARING OF FLOWERS

Flowers, "exquisite creatures" that they are, are beautiful always; but there are some cases where certain flowers, especially when worn by individuals, are more beautiful than others and a certain combination of flowers is more pleasing and expresses more individuality than another.

A young woman for whom I have the greatest admiration always plans the most unique color schemes in flowers that it has ever been my pleasure to see. It may be one rose in a vase or one rose on a gown, but it is just the right rose in size and color in exactly the right place, and it is more effective than a dozen would be when incorrectly used.

Once I saw this woman, whose eyes are as dark as night itself and whose hair is a very dark and beautiful brown, dressed in a dark-brown velvet gown simple in line, with just a plain piece of real lace in cream color at the neck coming down in a long line in the front. At the waist line, she wore one American Beauty rose with three green leaves. I wish you could picture how the long stem of the rose accentuated the long line of the collar and how the bit of color supplied that delightful touch which made the frock appear far above the ordinary.

If you are small in stature, trim in figure, and attractive in face, you can wear sweet-heart roses, Killarney roses, rosebuds, lilies of the valley, or any exquisite little bouquet made of dainty flowers. But if you are large in stature, dignified in posture, you should be very careful to wear exactly the right flower of exactly the right size in exactly the right place.

I know a tall girl who wears tobacco brown a very great deal. One time you will see her, probably at an afternoon function, wearing a corsage bouquet of violets, in the center of which she has placed a beautiful marigold, thus giving just the life to the costume that the purple of the violets fail to give. Again you may see her at a fashion opening or a luncheon with one beautiful yellow chrysanthemum on her brown tailored suit. One thing, though, I have always noticed is that no matter what color of flower she wears, she has just a harmonizing fleck of the "yellow-gold" to enchance the beauty of the brown of her costume.

One day I saw a beautiful one-piece gown in a select shop. It was a reseda-green crêpe The lines were as unpretentious as could be, but at the left-side front was a large fawn-brown velvet-and-linen rose with a long dark-green stem, the rose itself measuring possibly three and one-half inches in diameter Peeking out were three little buds with just a bit of chamois color, and at the neck was a collar of chamois color. The gown was wonderful. Why? Because it was simple, and each color was exquisitely in tune with the other.

Many beautiful color effects can be produced with artificial flowers, and such flowers are so simple and easy to make from bits of silk and ribbon and frequently so reasonable in price at the stores that when they are in fashion, you, as well as every other woman, may, if you choose, possess a suitable bouquet for every gown or suit.

But you must exercise care in selecting just the right color, just the right size, and just the right number for your bouquet. Sometimes, one wee bud or blossom is all that is necessary.

One time I saw a large woman with a beautiful beaver coat wearing one tiny white rose near her face, on the lapel. It was placed correctly and was of a suitable size to soften the coat around the face and give a desirable individual touch.

A prominent business woman of my acquaintance who wears severely tailored frocks —usualy a conventional blue serge—always uses a little stiff tailored rose or bud of some kind to lend color to her costume. She usually wears long white collars, and at the belt or on the shoulder she has a rose of very dark red—darker than the American Beauty—and sometimes this is backed up with a silver metal cloth, giving a stiff little flower that is in keeping with the tailored costume, but with just the touch of color that she feels she needs.

In wearing flowers, remember that some flowers, such as the old-fashioned garden flowers, are appropriate for summer dresses. Chrysanthemums, violets, and asters are appropriate to wear with suits and tailored garments. Orchids frequently are worn with suits, but they are not considered absolutely in good taste because of their frailty. For this reason, they are more frequently desired for wear with a beautiful evening gown or an afternoon frock. There are times, however, when orchids are beautiful with a suit. I remember of having seen a lavender orchid corsage bouquet worn with an exquisite gray velvet suit, not slate-gray nor mouse-gray, but an in-between gray, and it was just the right thing for that particular suit.

A GUIDE TO CORRECT DRESS FOR BUSINESS, OUTING, AND THE HOME—SPRING SEASON

Purpose	Dress	Hat	Coat	Gloves	Shoes	Accessories
Business, shopping, or walking.	One-piece dress of silk or wool, or blouse and separate skirt, semitailored; walking length.	Preferably close fitting; never extremely large; simple in effect.	Suit or light-weight cloak of becoming length, semitailored or strictly tailored and preferably of subdued color.	Rather heavy kid or fabric suede; tan, or to match suit.	High; medium weight; tan or black; lace or button; heels of medium height and size; walking shoes preferred.	Medium size bag, or pocketbook; preferably black or medium dark color.
Traveling.	Same as above.	Same as above.	Same as above.	Same as above.	Same as above.	Close-fitting veil and necessary traveling bag.
Motoring or outing.	Cloth suit with short skirt, semitailored; silk blouse and tailored skirt or one-piece dress of wool.	Very simple and close fitting; of soft felt, silk, leather, or kid.	Cravenette, flannel, or khaki; loose, long, or three-quarter length.	Tan cape, dogskin, or chamois.	High or low; low, firm heels; tan or black.	Change purse, vanity bag, and chiffon or silk mull veil.
Church, club meeting, or informal luncheon.	One-piece light-weight dress, or skirt to match jacket, with matching silk or light-lace, net, or chiffon blouse.	Becoming and simply trimmed, but more elegant than for business wear.	Suit or medium light-weight semitailored coat, of cloth or silk.	White kid, or to match suit.	High or low; plain kid or patent leather.	Small change purse; for elderly woman, silk or crocheted bag, in black or dark color, to hold purse, fan, and eye glasses.

Morning at home.	Simple washable dress or washable skirt and separate waist.	Hat to match garden frock of linen or rep.		Garden—leather or rubber.	Comfortable; high or low; black or tan.	Apron or cap, if work demands them.
Morning as a guest.	White washable skirt and separate waist, or pretty wash dress.		Knit sweater, or sport coat of wool or crash.		Same as above, or white or tan sport shoes.	Small work apron.
Afternoon at home.	Separate washable skirt and waist; simple one-piece dress.				Simple; good taste; black or colored shoes or slippers.	Small afternoon apron.
Afternoon as a guest.	One-piece dress of wool or silk; or white washable separate skirt and waist.				Same as for afternoon at home.	
Evening at home.	Same as afternoon; pretty silk for special occasions.				Same as for afternoon.	
Evening as a guest.	Same as for afternoon; or semievening or formal evening dress for special occasions, party, theater, or dance.			Long white or light-colored; silk or kid.	Black patent leather, or kid or satin to match dress.	Fan; scarf.

A GUIDE TO CORRECT DRESS FOR BUSINESS, OUTING, AND THE HOME—SUMMER SEASON

Purpose	Dress	Hat	Coat	Gloves	Shoes	Accessories
Business, shopping, or walking.	Light-weight wool or linen suit, with washable blouse; tailored linen, cotton, or washable silk dress.	Medium size; straw, or soft stitched fabric hat.	Unlined; three-quarter length, or shorter.	Washable; silk, lisle, or cotton.	High or low; black or tan; heels of medium size and height.	Medium size bag or pocketbook of fabric or leather; in black or colors.
Traveling.	Same as above.	Same as above.	Same as above.	Same as above.	Same as above.	Veil, umbrella, and traveling bag; rug and cushion, if necessary.
Motoring.	Dark silk or washable one-piece dress, or shirtwaist and suit.	Close-fitting fabric, straw hat or bonnet, or one of leather.	Medium-weight rain-proof; three-quarter or full length.	Washable cotton, kid, or chamois.	Same as above.	Veil, goggles, and fitted toilet bag or case.
Outing.	Same as for motoring.	Same as for motoring.	Same as for motoring, or sweater.	Same as for motoring.	Same as above, or white canvas or suède.	Parasol; walking stick.
Church, club meeting, or informal luncheon.	Dressy silk or fine cotton gown; silk suit, with a lace or chiffon waist.	Attractive, dressy hat, trimmed in any style and material that is becoming and comfortable.	Silk, satin, or fine light-weight cloth; three-quarter length or longer.	White, lisle, silk, or kid.	High or low; black, or to match suit or dress.	Fancy bag or pocketbook; fan; parasol.

Morning at home.	Simplest cotton one-piece dress.	Garden hat or bonnet.	Garden smock.		High or low; black, tan, or white.	
Morning as a guest.	Same as above, or white waist and skirt.	Same as above.	Same as above.		Same as above.	
Afternoon at home.	Same as for spring.	Same as for spring.			Same as for spring.	Same as for spring.
Afternoon as a guest.	One-piece dress of washable material, or white waist and skirt.	Same as for spring.			Same as for spring.	
Evening at home.	Sheer white or colored cotton, lace-trimmed dress.				Same as for spring.	
Evening as a guest.	Dressy white or colored cotton, attractively trimmed; thin silk, chiffon, lace, or net for special occasions.		Becoming, easy to slip on wrap of silk, voile, or similar wool fabric.	White; silk or kid.	Same as for spring.	Fan; scarf.

A GUIDE TO CORRECT DRESS FOR BUSINESS, OUTING, AND THE HOME
AUTUMN AND WINTER SEASONS

Purpose	Dress	Hat	Coat	Gloves	Shoes	Accessories
Business, shopping, or walking.	Serge, gabardine, broadcloth, or poplin one-piece dress or suit with matching or washable blouses	Small; becoming; felt, fabric, or velvet.	Easy fitting; three-quarter length, or longer; cheviot, broadcloth, or fabrics of similar weight; raincoat.	Kid, castor, or heavy fabric.	High; tan or black; heels of medium size and height. Rubbers.	Pocketbook or bag; silk muffler; furs; umbrella.
Traveling.	Same as above.	Same as above.	Same as above.	Same as above.	Same as above.	Same as above, with traveling bag, rug, and cushion, if necessary or desired.
Motoring or outing.	Plain-cloth one-piece dress, or heavy suit with separate waist.	Small; close-fitting; felt, fabric, leather, or kid.	Same as above.	Same as above.	Same as above.	Same as for business or shopping, without umbrella.
Church, club meeting, or informal lunch.	Cloth or velvet suit, with matching waist; dress of silk, velvet, or combination of silk and cloth.	Becoming trimmed hat; felt, velvet, or silk.	Cloth, velvet, or fur, in any becoming and fashionable length.	White, black, or matching kid.	High; black, plain, or patent leather; kid or cloth top.	Small bag or coin purse; face veil; fan.

Morning at home.	Heavy cotton dress, or washable waist and skirt.				High or low; black or tan.	Work apron.
Morning as a guest.	Simple cloth or cotton dress, or separate waist and skirt.				Same as for morning at home.	
Afternoon at home.	Attractive cloth or cotton dress; shirt-waist and skirt.				Same as for spring and summer.	Small afternoon apron.
Afternoon as a guest.	Rather dressy cloth or cotton dress; fancy blouse and separate skirt.	Becoming; felt, silk, or velvet.			Same as for spring and summer.	
Evening at home.	Same as afternoon; or pretty silk, if entertaining.				Black or colored kid slippers.	
Evening as a guest.	Same as afternoon; for special occasions, evening dress of silk, net, lace, chiffon, or fine fancy cotton.	Becoming and tastefully trimmed silk or chiffon hood.	Cloth or velvet wrap, or fur coat.	Long or short; white or matching kid.	Black or colored kid or satin slippers.	Fan; scarf; carriage slippers.

A GUIDE TO CORRECT DRESS FOR SPECIAL FUNCTIONS—ALL SEASONS

Purpose	Gown	Head Dress	Wrap	Gloves	Shoes	Accessories
Formal luncheon, day wedding, calling, or afternoon tea.	Dressy suit of fine cloth, silk, or velvet with matching waist; or, rather elaborate dress of cloth or silk or a combination of chiffon and silk or silk and cloth, probably white at the neck.	Becoming, dressy hat, of any fashionable size or shape.	Three-quarter or longer; silk, cloth, or velvet.	White kid; long or short, as the sleeves require.	Black, bronze, or matching kid; high or low.	Small, fancy bag; fan; face veil.
Informal dinner at home.	Any becoming silk or cotton gown.				Same as above.	
Informal dinner at restaurant or hotel.	Same as for formal luncheon, etc.	Same as above.	Practically same as above.	Practically same as above.	Practically same as above.	Practically same as above.
Formal dinner at home.	Simple, but becoming, evening dress.				Same as above.	Fan.
Formal dinner at restaurant or hotel.	Evening gown, slightly low in neck, or as for formal occasions; any style and color that is becoming.	No hat.	Silk or cloth coat or wrap.	White kid; long.	Kid or satin, to match gown.	Fan; scarf; opera bag.

Informal theater, concert, or lecture.	Practically same as for formal luncheon, etc.	Practically same as for formal luncheon, etc.	Practically same as for formal luncheon, etc.	Practically same as for formal luncheon, etc.	Practically same as for formal luncheon, etc.	Practically same as for formal luncheon, etc.
Formal theater, concert, or lecture.	Practically same as for formal dinner at restaurant.	Practically same as for formal dinner at restaurant.	Practically same as for formal dinner at restaurant.	Practically same as for formal dinner at restaurant.	Practically same as for formal dinner at restaurant.	Practically same as for formal dinner at restaurant.
Informal evening party.	Any simple, attractive, semievening dress of silk, net, lace, etc.		Cloth or silk.	White or color to match; silk or kid.	Black, bronze, or matching satin or kid slippers.	Scarf; fan; slipper bag.
Formal evening party.	Décolleté; black, white, or color; in silk, net, lace, or chiffon; may be very plain, if of handsome fabric, or trimmed.	Fancy comb. Matrons may wear feather ornament; girls, flowers, tulle, or ribbon.	Cloth or silk.	White or color to match; kid.	Same as above.	Same as above.
Formal ball or opera.	Practically same as above.	Practically same as above.	Practically same as above.	Practically same as above.	Practically same as above.	Practically same as above.

DRESSING APPROPRIATELY

So that you may form a more definite idea of what may be worn to advantage for business and outing and in the home, as well as what may be worn at special functions, I have arranged several guides in the form of tables These tables are intended simply to assist you in planning for yourself, and if you refer to them persistently and correctly interpret their contents you will derive much benefit from them.

The one relating to special functions is in the form of an all-season chart, because there is not a great difference between the several types of garments. In winter, heavier-weight materials and more brilliant colors are used than in spring and summer; also, more garments are provided, because, as a rule, there is more social life in the autumn and winter seasons.

What you should wear to the theater depends largely on the seat you are to occupy. It is perfectly correct to wear the same garments and accessories as is provided for Informal Theater if a theater box is to be occupied; and it is very much better taste to do so if the trip to the theater is not made in a private conveyance

Rather than slavishly follow the prevailing mode, you will find that the most beautiful, and decidedly the most practical, evening clothes are those which are designed to suit you, because they can be used for more than one season.

Formal dress should depend on the beauty of fabric and color, rather than on intricate style Informal evening dress is best when made of inexpensive fabrics, with more regard to design, for such garments are subject to harder usage than the more formal evening gowns, and as they are worn oftener they have shorter life.

If your circumstances are moderate, one evening wrap of conservative design, color, and fabric should serve you at least two years, and for all seasons except summer.

Garments of unlined silk or of knitted or crocheted silk or wool are acceptable for summer.

If you are not accustomed to attending many formal affairs and attend more afternoon than evening functions, you should select an afternoon coat of neutral tone or very dark shade, and a style and fabric equally suitable for afternoon and evening wear.

CULTIVATING INTELLIGENCE IN DRESS

I am giving here a few suggestions that, although seemingly commonplace, are of such practical value that they must be considered where appropriate or harmonious dress is concerned.

A dress may be ever so beautiful, yet, unless the individuality of the wearer and the accessories of the costume are in harmony with it, it will undoubtedly prove to be an expensive failure. Some women fail to realize the importance of this detail, thinking that if their frock is attractive the matter is ended, whereas an attractive frock is only one essential of good dress.

It would seem that, in a general way at least, nearly all women know that there is a law of eternal fitness in dress; yet not all have the taste and fine discrimination to apply the law unto themselves, few take the care that they should in selecting material suitable for certain occasions, and fewer still have any appreciation of color and style in design unless they are specially trained in this direction

It is true that no woman should wear materials of a color, design, or fashion that will in any way tend to exaggerate any marked characteristics or pecularities she may possess.

On the other hand, beauty of form and feature is generally sufficiently apparent not to necessitate calling attention to it by wearing garments that overemphasize these good qualities. Rather, an effort should be made to preserve the naturalness of these gifts and to show them in their greatest simplicity without making them brazenly conspicuous.

To dress correctly, you must have regard for the three forces of nature, namely, size, motion, and attraction There is a fitness of sentiment in dress that requires the exercise of care in the adaptation of style to the individual, holding ease, grace, and individuality as superior to all other considerations, and remembering always that beauty of form in dress is produced by the artistic combination of graceful curves growing out of each other, the lesser from the greater, the harmonious application of trimming, and the correct combination of colors, all of which tend to produce a oneness of effect that is pleasing to the eye and that gives poise and dignity to the wearer.

In material, design, and the arrangement of its parts, the main structure of a dress should be free from all unnecessary additions that will in any way interfere with its beauty of outline or gracefulness Accessories should be judiciously applied, as if growing from the most dominant parts or lines of a costume and thus emphasizing them If this thought is made to prevail throughout the trimming of a garment, it is possible to add force to the leading lines and develop a very harmonious display of coloring or line that will tastefully relieve any monotony of effect that might be characteristic of a severely plain dress.

As I have mentioned before, a piece of jewelry, such as a brooch or a necklace, will add much to the attractiveness of a bodice by giving tone or relieving plainness; yet these same ornaments may detract from the effect sought and even completely spoil it

Effects produced by harmony are much more pleasing and powerful than those produced by exaggerations, which at first shock and then oftentimes blunt one's appreciation of the purely artistic.

Women who have a strict regard for dress and ornament will avoid any inharmonious contrasts, and will never regard dress as a trivial or unimportant question. Dress is all important because it portrays character and individuality; therefore, to appear at your very best at all times, you must give due regard to appropriateness, comfort, gracefulness, and harmony.

To many, "French woman" is just another way of saying "the well-dressed woman" We marvel at her becoming way of dressing, no matter what her station or what the occasion —how she seems to carry a harmonious thought throughout her costume; and, yet, knowing this characteristic of the French woman, that she does suggest that which all women strive for—a pleasing appearance—we neglect to follow as closely as we should the thought she inspires.

Some claim that to dress well is a natural gift, and, to an extent, this is true. Nevertheless, women who are born without that quality which is so elusive and hard to define, and which is commonly called *taste,* need not despair, for with patience, study, observation, and application a very good idea as to the correctness and appropriateness of garments can be acquired.

Some women enthuse over certain colors They want them, they like to have them, and yet such colors may be the most trying of all colors for them. A woman possesses commendable control when she can deny herself the colors she likes best and wear those which are best suited to her type.

A good idea of the fitness of a color scheme in costume may be had from the following:

There were once two schoolgirls who looked very much alike They were of the same size and had the same coloring and general outline of feature. The mother of one often wondered why her daughter did not look so well dressed as the other girl. So one day she asked permission from the mother of the girl who looked very smart and attractive to copy her daughter's dresses, stating that she would use another color so that there would not seem to be such a sameness in the garments The girl who appeared smart and attractive wore an entire suit that was in absolute harmony; her accessories, her shoes, her hat, her coat—all were in accord with her dress Thus, one suit that she wore was simple in line and of smooth surface—brown material with a soft, cream blouse—and as accessories she wore a brown belt, brown gloves, brown shoes, and a cream-white straw hat trimmed with brown poppies. The other girl's mother, in her endeavor to have her daughter appear as attractive, duplicated this suit in blue, bought a light straw hat trimmed with red poppies, made blouses of various colors, and used gray gloves Thus she ignored absolutely any thought of harmony, and while her daughter's things were more expensive they were not effective. They lacked distinctiveness—discrimination; they lacked the well-dressed woman's knowledge and expression of color harmony.

In such failures as this lies a very good lesson—in fact, one of the secrets of dressing becomingly.

In every case, you must have a definite idea as to the extent of your wardrobe when you attempt to replenish it. If you know that brown and blue are your most becoming colors, you should decide which of these is best suited to the occasion or to the season and stick to this color, and, if possible, have accessories to correspond.

This way of dressing will also prove very economical if it is adhered to closely, for one pair of shoes, one pair of gloves, and one hat will often suffice for many occasions.

If your purse will not permit of more than one complete costume and you find that tailored clothes fit into your needs best, stick to them. Do not change over to fluffy things and then try to combine plain and fluffy clothes and expect to get a harmonious effect.

An overelaborate hat will spoil a tailored street suit, as will also shoes that are meant for indoor or party wear Heavy shoes are no more in keeping with an afternoon frock than are street gloves or a tailored hat.

A CLOTHES TRIUMPH

A physician with whom I am well acquainted—a capable, conscientious woman, skilled in her profession—had been so absorbed in her work that she never once considered the appropriateness of her clothing. This worked a handicap for her, because many people said that while she had demonstrated that she was a capable physician she was too frumpy in dress to impress one with her intelligence.

I like the doctor, and I appreciated her situation; also, I realized, when just hinting at the subject, that she, too, had been conscious of it for years.

She said, "I should like to be your patient and have you diagnose my case and plan clothes for me, just as I would diagnose your case and prescribe for you."

I agreed and "prescribed" clothes that I felt suited her exactly. She was deeply interested, and with her full cooperation the task was delightful.

She was as elated as a child when her associates remarked about the improvement in her clothes, and she told me that in less than two months there was a marked difference in the attitude of people toward her. Even the nurses in the hospitals had more admiration for her.

She realized that her word had more weight, more authority, even in her own household, and remarked that people who had not asked for her services before had called her in to administer to them.

She called it her clothes triumph, and said, "I have always been able to see that a well body and a well mind could go a long way toward making a person successful, but I never realized for an instant what a great factor clothes are until I had had this definite lesson."

The experience related occurred many years ago. This doctor is one of the best-dressed women in the prominent city in which she practices. She pays capable designers to plan her clothes, so that they fit her needs exactly, express her individuality, and are entirely in keeping with her position in her community.

CHAPTER IV

BECOMING DRESS

TRUTHS YOUR MIRROR TELLS—THE PROCESS OF ELIMINATION—LOOK YOUR BEST ALWAYS—CLOTHES FOR YOUR TYPE.

It takes very brave and sincere friends to be frank with us regarding the things that are becoming to us and those which are not What woman likes to be told truthfully that a dress she has labored over or paid more money for than she can afford is not becoming? Yet, many times, because we have not given the necessary time and study to the close relation of clothes to our individuality and personality, a dress we have dreamed of, labored over, and spent more for than we possibly should is a distracting failure!

When I was a child, I read a story about a little girl who had never looked in a mirror. Her hair was always tousled, and her dresses were always on awry and always soiled. To tell this little girl about her carelessness of herself had no effect until her teacher gave her a mirror. Then the teacher curled the little girl's hair, washed her face, and tidied her dress, and let her look in the mirror again. This told the child precisely what she should know—that she could be more attractive if she tried.

The value of a mirror in telling us of our shortcomings in dress is something many women do not appreciate. Do not stand before the mirror and comb your hair just to get the locks in place. Stand before it to study the contour of your face—use a triple mirror, if possible—and comb your hair to harmonize with the shape of your face and with your expression.

When you are planning a new dress, put on every dress in your wardrobe and analyze, in front of the mirror, the good points and bad points of each. In this way you will discern the becoming and the unbecoming points of each dress and so avoid mistakes, for they are mistakes Anything, that interferes with the harmonious costuming of your individual type is a mistake.

It frequently is said that girls in shops and offices dress more becomingly and in better taste than some women who spend three if not ten times as much for their clothes as does the office girl.

Why is this?

The woman of means may be attracted by a new fashion or a new color, and she buys it, regardless of whether or not it is becoming to her individual type.

The office girl cannot afford to buy the first dress she sees. She must select one or possibly two from several hundred, and, seeing the many dresses that she does each day, she, by a process of elimination, finds something that is appropriate for herself and, as a result, is pleasing to her associates.

Put your mirror in a good light, away from any shadows. Then study your face and figure, your eyes, your hair, and your complexion, so that you will know the truth. Mentally resolve that you will not buy anything that interferes with your determination to dress becomingly This at first may be as hard to practice as a diet for obesity, but it is worth the time and effort it takes if you expect to attain individuality and personal attractiveness.

LOOK YOUR BEST ALWAYS

If long lines in a dress are becoming to you, wear them; do not try to get an "all-ruffles-and-around" frock when you know that ruffles make you look stout and that you lack poise and grace in them.

A much respected woman who holds a prominent position in a large establishment did not for a long time realize the necessity of becoming clothes. Her clothes were selected without any thought, and were rarely appropriate or becoming. One day one of her associates told her she did herself an injustice by the haphazard way she selected her clothes, and suggested that she find a dressmaker who would study her type and design for her dresses that would express her individuality. The wisdom of this advice appealed to her and resulted in a visit to a reliable dressmaker Later, she appeared at the office in a delightful one-piece blue-serge frock that made her look twenty pounds lighter and ten years younger.

She laughs about it now, and says that before she had been at her desk a half hour, seven of her associates had told her they had never before seen her look so attractive. The foreman of the printery, who had known her and worked with her a number of years, came in and asked:

"Are you going away?"

"Why, no. Why?" she inquired.

"Well, I just had to ask, for I never saw you down here before with your 'Sunday dress' on."

So, you see, our associates do notice; and when we realize how much benefit we enjoy from being becomingly dressed, then we know that they, too, must appreciate seeing us in harmony with our surroundings.

Not long ago, a business man sent out for three girls who were engaged in the same line of work, and who seemed equally capable. He talked to them, and for promotion he selected a girl who wore a very plain but becoming and practical dress. Some one asked him why, and he replied:

"Well, she just seemed to fit into my needs. I know you thought I should choose Miss Blank, but she was too flamboyant. Her hair is too frumpy and she wears too much jewelry to suit me."

"What was wrong with the other girl? She has been here a little longer, you know."

"I don't just know," was the answer, "but the girl I selected will work out, I'm sure of that."

Later in the morning I had an opportunity to see the "other" girl, who was both pretty and capable. One glance told me that a soiled shirtwaist and a piece of gum had kept her from her opportunity.

CLOTHES FOR YOUR TYPE

Every woman and every girl should select costumes in absolute accord with her type; that is, in accord with her mentality, her environment, her duties, her pastimes, her coloring, her height, and her plumpness or thinness.

When the time is at hand to consider selecting, buying, or making clothes, put your whole mind on the problem. Ask yourself: Is it the correct thing for me? Is the color right? Are lines and the material right for my needs? Does it harmonize with other things I own? No matter whether it is hat, gown, coat, shoes, or purse, this last question should be asked, and then, after it is analyzed and found safe from every other point of view, do not select it unless it suits *your type.*

If you are attractive with buoyancy, express life and personal charm, and have a graceful body, wear clothes that seem to be overly modest, subdued, quiet, but simple, and express excellent taste.

A woman who has charm of personality and grace of figure needs but soft, subdued, inconspicuous clothing. By its simplicity and quietness, she may hold fast that charm which is so elusive and so easily covered up or "shooed away" by flamboyant dress.

A beautiful painting expressing life, with soft, exquisite coloring, has its beauty emphasized by a frame so simple that it is not even noticed by you while you "drink in" the beauty of the picture. And so it must be with the charming, vivacious girl or woman. But, remember, it takes more study, more work, more effort, to make a simple frame, a simple gown, beautiful than it does a fussy one, for you can keep on adding and adding to the others until you have a mass of construction. But try to eliminate and you will quickly see that elimination should have been begun at the moment the garment was conceived and carried out faithfully throughout the development.

To bring out simplicity of dress successfully means that the process of elimination must be begun before the material is selected Use only just what is right, and then let each line of the garment express individuality, not conspiracy against the line that joins it.

I recently had occasion to study the types right in my own offices. One day, one of the girls, who is attractive with buoyancy, and who is very close to me in my work, wore a dress that made her look broad-shouldered, short-waisted, and long from the waist line to the skirt hem. I thought about her dress several times, as I really had not been conscious of her clothes before, her personality having always dominated them entirely. Then I decided that the "little blue dress with its indefinite waist line and girlish collar" was the kind of dress for her type.

The next day this girl came to me saying, "Can you spare me a moment just for myself? I want to ask you about a little office dress. I have selected some pictures that I believe you will like."

We looked them over and found the dress that suited her particularly. It seemed just the thing, a beautiful frame for the vivaciousness expressed in her brightly lighted face and buoyant step. It was a modest little frock, to be made of dark-blue smooth-surface cloth, with a white collar that was long in the front and round and sort of "Dutchy" in the back, to give a youthful effect across the shoulders.

Deciding upon that dress set me thinking of each girl who came to my office that day, and I could not resist making mental notes of their costumes.

One girl came, so demure and shy and slight in figure (she is always so meek that I feel I must give her immediate consideration lest she run away). For her, the little blue frock would not do at all. I noticed that her dress was particularly becoming. It was deep red, nearer a burgundy, but just red enough to give a pink flush to a face so fair that it was almost pallid. The dress was simple, but the lines very interesting. I turned back my thought clock just for a moment and remembered that when I first saw her she wore a pretty dark-red sweater that was "different" and decidedly becoming, and I remembered very well just how it was knitted, emphasizing that she realized, as all women should, the importance of individuality in her dress. Even in her sweater she had secured interesting lines that were expressive of her.

The next one to come was one full of life, of vim, and petite in face and figure. To express her type, she needs clothes that are smart, that have "snap" to them. She is able to wear Dame Fashion's most extreme creations, and wear them well You will be able to picture her better when I tell you that one time, when she was helping to dress a model for a fashion exhibition, one of the manikins put on a smart hat in such a lackadaisical way that it looked positively dowdy This little "vim" girl walked up to her, and, without even thinking, took hold of the hat, tilted it slightly, brought it down over her forehead, and said:

"To be truly smart, you must always put your hat on 'with a splash'."

A young woman expressing dignity in her manner and dress came into my office next. She was wearing a black soft-silk dress simple in design and having a white collar so spotlessly clean that it seemed to bear out the dignity of the wearer. Her genuine smile and womanliness seemed, if possible, to be overemphasized by the simplicity of her costume.

Each year that we live, we should grow and develop with experience, and we will if we are receptive and interested and grateful for the privilege of living. If we are successful, we must acquire poise and outwardly express our intelligence. These two qualities produce dignity, and as we acquire dignity in manner we show it in our dress.

A woman of forty, on the street or in the office, cannot under any circumstances wear the same type of blouses, shoes, and hats that a young girl can. A great many women have a wrong idea about this, and feel that to appear young—and where is the woman who has not this desire?—they must wear youthful clothes. This is a grave mistake.

If you are forty or more, remember that in wearing clothes that are too youthful for you, you lose your background and you have nothing to aid you in concealing the age that your face and figure evidence.

A woman who has been going to business for five years will always display better taste in dress than one who is in her first business year. Why? Because she has learned from experience that she cannot, from a money-and-time point of view, wear frivolous clothes.

My advice to you, no matter what your type may be, is this: Wear nothing that attracts more than your personality, for then the value of *you* would be lost.

One time, under a picture in a magazine, I read this inscription: "It seems so funny to look back at the styles. They are always so misfit after they have gone by."

I thought over these words a considerable time, then I realized that to a very great extent they are true. Clothes are many times put together without definite thought, without regard for type, and when the immediate time of their wearing has passed, they are nothing short of grotesque.

In reasoning this out further, I took from my bookcase several volumes on historic dress and looked over the pictures. Some of the costumes were beautiful. Those which were beautiful would be just as attractive today as they were the day they were worn. I then thought of women whom I knew whose clothes will live

My mind saw a vision of Mary Pickford—Mary Pickford, one of the most successfully dressed artists of this age. I say most successfully, because Mary Pickford makes her clothes express youth in every line—youth that makes her and her work a wonderful triumph

The pictures in which Mary Pickford's costumes have a prominent part will live for an indefinite time because of the simplicity, quaintness, and charm that is carried out to the minutest detail in every one of them. She never follows a definite fad or fancy, but selects clothes that are becoming to her individuality—to her type—clothes that are in keeping with the parts she plays

We play a part in every-day life, just as Mary Pickford plays on the screen; but often we do not realize that we have a part—a part in dressing appropriately and becomingly for everything we do, so that we will make a picture that is pleasing to all who come in contact with us—a picture that will long remain in the thoughts of our friends.

MARY PICKFORD

Whose clothes express the charm of youth

Photo by Hartsook

CHAPTER V

YOUR COLOR

A STUDY OF COLOR—THE COLOR FAMILY—COLOR NAMES —DEVELOPMENT OF COLOR SENSE—COLOR CHARACTERISTICS AND COMBINATIONS—SELECTING YOUR COLOR—COLORS FOR VARIOUS TYPES.

I am going to talk to you about color—your color—in this chapter. A lesson in color is interesting and helpful. The very principles of distinctive dress embrace color, lines, and fabric, and one should never underestimate the important part they play in the matter of successful costuming.

Manufacturers and shopkeepers agree that a certain design may be very successful in a certain color and fabric but an absolute failure in another. Therefore, to use colors pleasingly and blend them harmoniously, one must understand them.

It is a recognized fact among salespeople that color is what first attracts a customer's attention, particularly in wearing apparel. The color of a gown or a suit is invariably decided before the kind or quality of fabric is considered.

Color expresses and signifies emotions, both physical and mental, a fact that may be verified by looking to nature, to the changes of color brought about by the changing seasons. Thus, the green of spring denotes freshness, youth, purity, and hope; the brilliant, glowing colors of summer are symbols of vigorous, ardent motherhood; the somber tones of autumn portray the richness and beauty of a successful maturity; and winter with its brown-gray trees, gray skies, and snowy whiteness, typifies the graciousness and tolerance of age.

Again color has been called the "music of light." The significance of this expression may be readily grasped by persons who have learned to see and to use color intelligently. Thus, the fundamental, or foundation, colors may be likened to the notes of a musical instrument—a piano, for instance. Both the variations and harmonious combination of color are easily compared to the harmonies produced on the piano by a skilful, studied combination of the notes of a musical scale. Likewise, the light shades, the incidental or indefinite qualities of color, may be compared or considered as would these same values in a musical composition, grouped to produce a pleasing sound or a pleasing spectacle.

You may study color in two general ways. One way is by association—that is, by becoming so familiar with the various color combinations from actual observation as to be able to tell beforehand what the general effect will be. This knowledge is generally obtained by observing and associating with objects whose chief beauty lies in their coloring.

The other way is by studying the laws and principles governing harmonious combinations that have been formulated by persons who have made a special study of this subject.

By practicing the former method you may develop a fine sense of color; but without any theoretical knowledge the color combination will be limited to the copying of certain pleasing color effects that may be observed in art or in nature.

Once the laws and principles of color are clearly fixed in your mind, the combining of colors to bring out the best effects in dress can be done with confidence, and it is work that will grow more fascinating the more deeply you enter into it

The practical application of the theory of color has not kept pace with many of the other branches of art and industry. This is not because its study has not been persistently and successfully followed by scientists, but because those of their investigations which have been made available for the artizan are looked upon as being of doubtful value for practical purposes

It is a common idea that the faculty of so combining colors as to produce artistic results is less a question of science than of a certain inborn taste, and that unless one possesses this peculiar gift it is of little use for him or her to attempt any color combinations

That certain persons possess a decided taste for color, or, as it is commonly termed, "an eye for color," is beyond question. Parallel cases are found in the field of music, where certain individuals have a most pronounced gift for placing chords and memorizing melodies But a lack of these particular talents in either field will not prevent you from gaining satisfactory results.

THE COLOR FAMILY

There are three primary colors: red, blue, and yellow

Some noted artists in working with them said there should be seven colors, all the colors of the rainbow: purple (violet), indigo, blue, green, yellow, orange, and red.

A close study of Fig. 2 will show first the three primary colors; and then, by the combining of these three colors, how other colors, called secondary colors, are produced.

In Fig. 1, I am showing you a scale of colors with red, yellow, and blue—1, 3, and 5 —as a base and with the secondary colors, orange, green, and violet—2, 4, and 6. These colors may be further identified by R for red, O for orange, Y for yellow, G for green, B for blue, and V for violet.

To know color, you should first become thoroughly familiar with the three primary colors: red, yellow, and blue. Then you should learn how these may be combined to make the seven colors. Thus, red and yellow, two colors, make orange, a third color; yellow and blue, two colors, make green, a third color; blue and red make violet; and red, yellow, and blue make indigo, which is the only one of the combinations that is not considered as a secondary color.

Again, go back to Fig. 1. Think of the scale as cylindrical in form, as though you had it cut out and were holding it up in your hand as a circle. You will see then clearly that the connecting hues between red and violet are omitted.

Consider red as your base. There are two kinds of red, red-yellow and red-blue (The three red-blue colors, or shades, between red and violet are omitted from the scale through necessity of the black background. They are, however, red-red-violet, red-violet, red-violet-red, and should be considered in connection with the study of this scale.) Red-yellow is red in combination with a smaller quantity of yellow. Red-blue is red in combination with a smaller quantity of blue. The first color mentioned is the predominating color.

Next, consider yellow as your base. Yellow in combination with a small amount of red gives yellow-orange; in combination with a small amount of blue, yellow-green. Blue with a little red gives blue-violet; blue with a little yellow gives blue-green.

Study the color scale. Be sure that you understand first the three colors, then the seven. Then fix in your mind definitely that from these colors emanate all other colors

Red extends two ways on the scale, into blue and into yellow. The colors extending to a point half way between red and blue and half way between red and yellow would come in the family of red, because they have red as a base. But to you, a woman, it would seem unfair to class all these beautiful shades and tints of red as red, although from a fine sense of color they are You do not think of pink, flesh, orange, and even russet as red, yet they are of the same family, the same as blue-violet and blue-green are of the family of blue.

All the beautiful tones and hues of color should be appreciated.

It is very necessary in order to appreciate colors fully that you should know about color tones. Tones are developed by the addition of black for shades and white for tints.

It is necessary, too, that you should have a clear idea of hue, and this is shown in Fig. 1, which is really a scale of spectrum hues. If to a color is added a small amount of another color, a change in hue is produced. Thus, a little orange added to red gives red-red-orange, a hue of red It is the hue of a color that often makes it becoming or unbecoming, a point that is well worth remembering.

When a color is suggested as becoming to you, make sure that you understand from what basic color it came You might be able to wear, for instance, red-violet, which would be a soft plum color, but you may not have enough color and vivaciousness to wear blue-violet. You must see and realize that there are two distinct kinds of violet color, just as there are two kinds of blues, two greens, two yellows, two oranges, and two reds, and think of them in two colors, not just as blue, green, red, and violet.

COLOR COMBINATIONS

Principal Color		Perfect	Excellent	Strong	Good	Fair	Weak
Blue	Light	Cream	Light brown	Yellow	Olive green	Pink	Purple
	Medium	Cream	Medium brown	Yellow	Medium green	Medium red	Lavender
	Dark	Gold	Dark brown	Orange	Medium green	Medium red	Heliotrope
Brown	Light	Cream	Light blue	Myrtle green	Shell pink	Nile green	Purple
	Medium	Cream	Light blue	Medium green	Salmon pink	Reseda	Gray
	Dark	Gold	Turquoise blue	Medium orange	Rose pink	Medium red	Lavender
Drab	Light	Light blue	Salmon pink	Medium green	Red	Heliotrope	Cream
	Medium	Medium blue	Rose pink	Medium green	Wine	Lavender	Gray
	Dark	Dark blue	Rose pink	Dark green	Maroon	Purple	Yellow
Gray	Light	Light blue	Rose pink	Medium green	Red	Lavender	Cream
	Medium	Medium blue	Salmon pink	Medium green	Wine	Heliotrope	Tan
	Dark	Dark blue	Salmon pink	Dark green	Maroon	Purple	Brown
Green	Light	Light cream	Delicate pink	Purple	Wine	Medium gray	Light blue
	Medium	Medium cream	Rose pink	Yellow	Medium red	Navy blue	Light blue
	Dark	Medium gold	Rose pink	Orange	Dark red	Medium lavender	Light blue
Lavender	Light	Light purple	Delicate pink	Light brown	Medium gray	Light green	Yellow
	Medium	Light purple	Rose pink	Medium tan	Pale blue	Medium green	Red
	Dark	Dark purple	Ivory white	Dark brown	Light blue	Medium green	Maroon

Maroon	Light	Cream	Light blue	Light yellow	Medium green	Medium tan	Scarlet
	Medium	Silver	Medium blue	Medium yellow	Medium green	Medium tan	Purple
	Dark	Gold	Medium blue	Medium orange	Dark green	Medium gray	Lavender
Orange	Light	Purple	Medium blue	Light green	Light brown	Gold	Yellow
	Medium	Purple	Medium blue	Medium green	Light brown	Gold	Cream
	Dark	Purple	Medium blue	Dark green	Medium red	Silver	Lavender
Pink	Light	Light blue	Lavender	Light tan	Light gray	Light green	Scarlet
	Medium	Medium blue	Heliotrope	Medium tan	Medium gray	Medium green	Red
	Dark	Medium blue	Purple	Medium brown	Medium gray	Medium green	Dark blue
Purple	Light	Lavender	Light green	Light yellow	Cream	Salmon pink	Red
	Medium	Heliotrope	Medium green	Medium yellow	Silver	Rose pink	Scarlet
	Dark	Lavender	Medium green	Orange	Gold	Medium gray	Scarlet
Red	Light	Cream	Light tan	Medium green	Light blue	Light yellow	Purple
	Medium	Silver	Light tan	Olive green	Navy blue	Medium yellow	Lavender
	Dark	Gold	Light brown	Dark green	Dark blue	Medium orange	Pink
Yellow	Light	Purple	Light brown	Light blue	Light green	Salmon pink	Cream
	Medium	Purple	Medium brown	Navy blue	Medium green	Rose pink	Silver
	Dark	Purple	Dark brown	Dark blue	Dark green	Heliotrope	Gray

NOTE.—In using this table as a reference to harmonious and distinctive dress, it is well to bear in mind fabric colors, tones, and shades as regulated by seasonal and style changes rather than artists' colors, so that a conception of correct combinations will result.

A woman whom I know well, whose eyes are brown and whose hair is red-brown, can wear any of the yellow or orange browns and can wear green-yellow perfectly, but blue-green gives her a lifeless, tired look, demonstrating that life in the color, when a definite color is used, is required for her particular type

This same woman wears dark blue well, for the reason that there is no interference from the color of her frock, and her eyes, hair, and complexion dominate over the dark blue and supply that which the blue-green color tends to "kill."

In the table shown on pages 120 and 121, I have arranged a large number of color combinations that will serve to guide you in assembling colors This table may be used freely, and while it does not cover all known colors you will find that it has sufficient combinations to simplify the selection of colors for dress.

COLOR NAMES

To obtain a good knowledge of the various color names that are applied to materials for dress, you will make no mistake in referring to the color cards issued from time to time by dealers in such materials, as well as by textile manufacturers and dyers

So many of these cards have been issued and so many different names have been applied to colors that are alike that an attempt at standardizing the various colors has been made by various concerns that have united to form what is officially called The Textile Color Card Association of the United States, Incorporated.

This association has issued cards that should eventually prove valuable not only to manufacturers, but to dealers and individuals as well, for the colors are so numbered that it will be possible to match all materials and threads by number, provided the number assigned to colors by this association are adopted by all textile and allied industries.

To give you an idea of the manner in which this association has gone about this matter, I might state that a system of standard numbers has been established giving each color a number consisting of four figures that expresses as nearly as can be done the character of the color according to the following plan:

The first, second, and third figures indicate the relative proportions of the component parts of a color. Thus, the first figure indicates the principal color on which the shade is based, the second the principal blend, and the third the secondary blend. For the purpose of identification, white is numbered 1; red, 2; orange, 3; yellow, 4; green, 5; blue, 6; violet, 7; gray, 8; black, 9; and no change, 0. The fourth figure of the color number indicates the strength of the color designated by the first three figures. To the lightest is assigned the number 1; to the second lightest, 2; to light, 3; medium light, 4; medium, 5; medium dark, 6; dark, 7; second darkest, 8; and darkest, 9. In addition the abbreviation S., for standard, or O., for season number, is prefixed to the color number in order to avoid possible interference with established numbers.

To illustrate the system devised by this association, let us consider the color turquoise, to which is assigned the number S. 6153. As you will observe, 6 represents blue, the principal color; 1, white, the principal blend; 5, green, the secondary blend; and the last number, 3, the light strength.

Following is a list of the standard color numbers issued by this association, together with the name applied in each case:

1001	White	2007	Dark Cardinal
1041	Ivory	2009	Garnet
1045	Cream	2035	Geranium
2003	Scarlet	2063	Cherry
2005	Cardinal	2065	Ruby

2067	American Beauty	4285	Terra Cotta
2103	Pink 1	4287	Mahogany
2105	Pink 2	4383	Chamois
2107	Pink 3	4815	Gold
2131	Flesh	4817	Old Gold
2145	Salmon Pink	5005	Emerald
2163	Wild Rose	5007	Hunter
2165	Raspberry	5067	Myrtle
2167	Claret	5143	Nile Green
2169	Burgundy	5164	Ocean Green
2174	Ashes of Roses	5183	Mignonette
2183	Old Rose	5185	Reseda
2185	Strawberry	5385	Bronze
3005	Orange	5413	Chartreuse
3025	Burnt Orange	5485	Olive
3083	Tan	5495	Evergreen
3115	Maize	5823	Sage
3183	Écru	5827	Bottle Green
3185	Fawn	6005	National
3187	Beaver	6007	Yale Blue
3285	Gold Brown	6053	Saxe Blue
3295	Brown	6055	Electric
3485	Topaz	6057	Sapphire
3842	Buff	6083	Marine
3925	Chestnut	6085	Navy
3928	Seal	6103	Light Blue 1
3945	Tobacco	6105	Light Blue 2
3948	Negro	6107	Light Blue 3
4005	Lemon	6109	Light Blue 4
4025	Golden Rod	6123	Cornflower
4115	Leghorn	6153	Turquoise
4123	Apricot	6183	Copenhagen
4183	Champagne	6185	Delft
4185	Beige	6505	Peacock

6853	Cadet	7205	Fuchsia
6855	Regimental	7285	Magenta
6925	Navy 2	7814	Heliotrope
6875	Navy 3	7817	Prune
6985	Midnight	7905	Egg Plant
7003	Violet	8065	Steel
7005	Pansy	8067	Slate
7007	Purple	8111	Pearl Gray
7123	Lavender	8113	Silver
7163	Lilac	8115	Nickel
7183	Orchid	8843	Castor
7195	Amethyst	8845	Taupe
7187	Plum	8935	Smoke
7195	Wisteria	8965	Graphite

DEVELOPMENT OF COLOR SENSE

With the principles of color understood, you may readily turn to the application of color in dress, so that appropriate color schemes for given purposes may be developed. The ways in which to become familiar with color combinations are numerous.

Once you have become sufficiently experienced to define hues, tints, and shades, and have trained your eye to observe and your memory to retain normal colors with their variations, you will be able to learn much from nature's combinations, be it in cloud and atmospheric effects, autumn tint and foliage, flowers, minerals, animals, birds, insects, and so on.

Then, by visiting museums and exhibitions, you may study effects in china, glass, and textiles, including tapestries, rugs, and old embroideries and laces; or by frequenting the art galleries, you may gain inspiration from old and new Japanese prints and from the exhibits of old and new masters in art.

Again, the ballroom, automobile shows, and other places where variety and gaiety in dress may be seen will help to give you ideas of color, to say nothing of the theater and even the motion-picture playhouses, where old-period gowns and other equally interesting styles and colorings are often portrayed.

You may also get inspiration from the beautiful colors in the shops and show windows. Indeed, many a beautiful gown has been created by designers who, having seen some beautiful creation, were inspired to apply their knowledge of color, line, and fabric.

Taste in color is largely a matter of civilization and cultivation. The nearer a person approaches the savage, the greater is the inclination for brilliant colors; yet it is true that many excellent effects are attained by savage races. As civilization advances, the reverse is true, the colors being less severe and leaning more to the soft, quiet tones, in imitation of nature.

Nature has given to each of us a keynote of color. It is helpful to study and fully appreciate her judicious and well-proportioned uses, and it is interesting to know that she uses but comparatively small quantities in proportion to her range of the intense or bright colors. Her greens, grays, and browns are enlivened by but small touches of blue, red, orange, and other bright colors.

It is always best, as far as possible, to preserve Nature's proportions when following her suggestions. Once, when asked regarding appropriate dress by a ponderous woman who was dressed in red velvet, a prominent lecturer on dress harmony made this reply: "Madam, Nature made some butterflies and some humming birds red, but she made elephants taupe, and Nature, madam, serves as a good color criterion." This answer is a wise though somewhat curt illustration, emphasizing the fact that brilliant colors must be used in small quantity, and shades in bulk.

Some of the color combinations most frequently met with in nature are the white and yellow of the daisy; the brown and yellow of the sunflower; the yellow and purple of the pansy; the light salmon, yellowish green, cream, and moss-green of the tea rose, which affords an ideal suggestion for a combination of delicate tints; the American beauty rose, with its hues from violet to red, together with the tones of green in the leaves. The nasturtium, with its tones of yellow and orange and its tender green foliage, is a fine example of combining warm colors. A bunch of grapes, with its various catawba shades, or shaded from green to blue and violet, is also full of suggestions. Then there are the browns, pinks, greens, rose pinks, reds, and grays of the autumn leaves as a source of inspiration. So the list might be extended indefinitely by exercising the faculty of observation.

COLOR CHARACTERISTICS AND COMBINATIONS

To become familiar with the colors used in dress, look into their characteristics.

Blue may be regarded as a standard color for woman's dress. It not only gives the impression of coolness, but is restful and unobtrusive The lighter tints are very closely related to white, and when it is the purpose to make white give the impression of purity a bluish tint is always given to it. On the other hand, when mixed with black, blue produces a black that gives the impression of greater blackness Blue frequently is preferred to black, because it is not inclined to look grayish in combination with some of the other colors.

Every season brings its new range of colors. Many new colors—some queer, some positively ugly—are presented as being the very latest and, of course, the most fashionable colors. The various exploiters of fashion proclaim each color as desirable, but invariably, after all is said, the assertion is made that blue is good and will be worn, thus emphasizing the power of popular demand.

Blue is always fashionable, because women instinctively understand its value as a garment color, and it predominates because it best enhances the good points of the wearer, in both the figure and the complexion. It does not by its intensity or depth obliterate the real charm of the face or form; neither does it accentuate any unpleasing features

White in its different varieties, the same as blue, may be called a standard, because it, too, is universally becoming, but the same thing cannot be said of black. Black is not becoming to nor desirable for all women, as it emphasizes age and adds as many years to a face as white will subtract from it A prominent writer credits the French women with saying that black should not be worn after a woman is thirty, unless for mourning, nor again until after she is sixty, and then only if she feels that she has to wear it.

Violet is more pliable in its combinations than some of the other colors. It associates well with green-yellow, yellow-green, orange, orange-yellow, yellow, gold, gray, and green, but rarely is it satisfactory with red or blue, unless some intermediate tone or a neutral color is used with it

The darkest shades of orange form pleasing combinations with subdued yellows, especially when a stripe or a small figure of black is worked into the material. Light orange is too bright to be used freely, but yellow-orange or gold can be used to good advantage for embellishments

Green is very restful to the eye and forms an agreeable harmony with white Its effect is to lend brilliancy Light greens upon dark grounds produce pleasing effects, while the reverse is less satisfactory. Light and grayish greens are desirable in plain materials or as stripes, figures, or borders of darker tone. Blue-green, however, is difficult to combine with other colors, combining best with gold and with red in small quantities.

When you combine colors, you must be careful not to injure the purity of one by an excess of another. For instance, light blue and light pink go well together, because neither is sufficiently intense to overpower the other. But an equal quantity of light blue and normal red will not harmonize, because the greater intensity of the red will overpower the blue and make it look sickly or faded

Thus, it will be seen that when the intensity of colors differs greatly, the quantity of each that is used must also differ in order to produce a combination that is harmonious; that is, the intense color must be used in much smaller quantity as a trimming or outline to the lighter one in a given color scheme.

As I have stated before, colors that contrast harshly may be blended into harmony by placing intermediate hues, tones, or the neutrals between them. Thus, black, white, or gray between strong, bright colors neutralize them and prevent confliction. Very bright colors in quantity are detrimental to somber ones when placed side by side.

SELECTING YOUR COLOR

If you select the right colors for your dress, everybody concerned derives satisfaction from your intelligent choice.

Most persons experience real pleasure or displeasure from colors, some claiming that certain colors affect them to the extent that they cause happiness or depression, according to the way in which the individual views them.

It is claimed, too, that right color in one's dress has a beneficial effect on the health of the body and the mind of both the wearer and the observer. Indeed, it cannot be disputed that different colors produce different effects on the individual—that they excite different and varying states of feeling. This undoubtedly accounts for the pleasure and comfort so often experienced in wearing some particular garment.

A regrettable thing, however, is that we can seldom define this feeling or credit it to the proper cause; it is unfortunate, too, that the effect of color on different persons is as widely different as the effect of musical sound, for just as there are persons devoid of sound appreciation, that is, with no ear for music, so there are persons without a color sense, a defect that is usually designated as color blindness or color ignorance.

The lack of this faculty, fortunately, is less frequently found in women than in men, and this may be attributed to the fact that with the advance of civilization men have practically discarded color in its broad uses, whereas women have clung to color, not only for their dress, but for their home decoration

One of the natural and God-given duties of woman is to charm and please, and color rightly used is a wonderful factor in accomplishing this end.

If I were asked to give a color standard for woman's dress that could be adhered to continuously, I would have to confess that it is practically impossible. Each season produces new shades, tints, or tones of colors that cannot be classified, and these may put at variance any method that might be worked out during a previous season.

Of course, if the advice of advocates of a standard type of dress for women were followed, it might be possible to plan garments for them in much the same manner as men's garments are planned. While much may be said for and against the adoption of such a standard type of dress, its discussion here is not warranted; yet I must emphasize that such a style would have a tendency to take away from woman the privilege she has of bringing out her best points. As matters now stand, there is much unattractive color in woman's dress; yet how much more displeasing, yes, even distressing, might be the effect if we could wear no colors save the somber blacks, blues, browns, and grays that constitute the color range of men's clothes.

Color is and should be made to express personality.

Often it is made to do this only crudely, even offensively; and too often it serves to express but the foolish desire to attract attention or to be attired in what is considered the latest fashion.

Color should charm and delight the observer and fit in most harmoniously with surroundings; it should be an expression of one's best thoughts

Love of color is not to be condemned, for color should be made the means of enhancing real beauty of face and form and an aid in clarifying and idealizing plain features of face and figure. Too often it is allowed to lessen the effect of real beauty and to accentuate ugliness or plainness of feature.

In selecting color for yourself, you must always make sure of whether or not it suits your individuality. Do not rush headlong after the newest color on the counter simply because it is new, although in this respect I feel safe in saying that a sufficient number of colors are brought out each season to suit all types and to meet all demands.

Personal coloring depends on health and happiness, as well as on sickness and sadness, so that a shade or a tint that is becoming to you at one time may be found very trying at another. Besides, you should take into consideration the color and texture of your skin, and the color of your eyes and hair. Particularly should you follow this advice if Nature is beginning to dim the color and brilliancy of your eyes and to turn the natural color of your hair to gray or white. Under such circumstances a readjustment of color is advisable. The tint or the shade must be varied; that is, lighter or darker tones should, almost invariably, be resorted to

Brilliant, hard, cold colors, or what might be fittingly termed unrelenting or non-retiring colors, should be avoided once a woman is past her first youth; in fact, not every young woman or young girl can afford to wear such tones. For instance, pure blue, red, or yellow, grass green, the popular golf red, and similar colors that are launched forth nearly every season as being the latest thing are so strong that they rob the wearer of all the natural color of skin, hair, and eyes, making even a young, vigorous girl appear devoid of animation and charm.

The use of such colors even as trimming is a mistake commonly made by women lacking in the natural color of skin, hair, and eyes, such women unquestionably believing that because of their own lack of color it is the correct thing to do.

You will do well to note that gray eyes reflect blue or green, and sometimes brown tints, and that the right shade of blue will increase the color and brilliancy of blue eyes.

Blue face veils give the effect of having clarified the skin and heightened the color, and are for this reason a pleasing accessory to many women's toilets. Face veils of white, however, should be avoided except by the very youthful and those having a clear, highly colored complexion.

It is important that you consider your eyes, hair, and skin in choosing colors for your dress, being careful to avoid those which will give you a faded, unhealthy tinge, or too harsh and florid an appearance, and choosing that which will enhance the beauty of your individual coloring.

Your attention is called to the surprising changes that are brought about in a person's appearance by light showing through colored fabrics, especially those used in gaily colored parasols A green parasol makes red hair appear brown; violet eyes, bluish-green brown; red lips, brown; white skin, green; black gloves, greenish-brown; and a green coat, deeper green. An orange parasol makes a snow-white forehead appear orange colored; rosy cheeks, scarlet; red lips, scarlet; the neck and skin where the reflected light strikes, orange; yellow gloves, yellow-orange; and a black coat, maroon.

The lining in coats should have consideration. Many women like beautiful linings, and in the linings of their coats indulge this fancy to their hearts' content But great caution should be exercised in selecting a coat lining, so that when it is thrown back in a theater, in a hotel dining room, or in any place where it will be seen, the lining will make a suitable background for you and your gown Many times the color of the lining may be such that it will be very effective and add much to the "picture," but if it is of a jarring color, the effect may be entirely spoiled.

You may be interested to know, too, that color in dress materials is affected by light, all colors being lessened or increased in richness, brilliancy, or beauty according to whether they are seen in daylight or under artificial light. Therefore, in selecting colors for evening garments, you will profit by examining the materials under artificial light and those for day wear in daylight

In selecting silent-tone fabrics, you will likewise do well to avoid the influence that other colors or more brilliant hues exert. For instance, if you desire a very dark blue, take the material where other colors will not detract from it, and in this way its real tone and color will assert itself. Very often a soft, beautiful color will be killed by being placed close to a color that is more brilliant.

Still another factor that you should reckon with in the selection of color is its seasonal adaptability Shakespeare's advice to actors to "suit the action to the word" might well be paraphrased in advice to women to "suit the color to the season."

Climate and season are closely related to the color and weight of garments, and they demand considerable thought if one is to be appropriately and artistically dressed.

It is indeed distressing to see a woman dressed in red, warm brown, yellow, or orange on a warm day in June or July. Although beautifully glowing in winter weather, such colors are shunned by the tasteful dresser in warm weather. Instead, she will wear gowns and hats of white and light tints, of blue and its related colors, green and violet, and other cool colors, so as not to produce a sense of warmth or heat.

Nature, as I have already remarked, serves as an excellent guide in color selection, and she may always be followed to advantage in matters of dress.

In the spring, Old Mother Nature does not consult the fashion books, but puts forth the beautiful violets, primroses, hyacinths, and daffodils. In her scheme of coloring she harmonizes the fresh green of the trees with the pink petals of the apple blossoms and the delicate coloring of the springtime flowers. Her color scheme is so near perfection that no one has been clever enough to improve on it. In summer, she modifies these colors, making them less brilliant, thereby creating an atmosphere of coolness and comfort; in autumn she turns the foliage to the soft browns, tans, and russets, suggesting appropriate colors for this season; and as snowy, bleak, cold winter steals upon us, she warns us to defy the icy blasts by dressing warmly and putting on bright colors suggestive of heat and warmth.

Black and cold gray, which display no cheerfulness, are colors given over to sorrow, calmness, and the passing out of this world. They are not appropriate for the joy manifested at the dawn of spring, when everything in Nature's garden thrills with happiness. White, however, is always symbolic of purity and repose, is ever dear to us, and is most often worn in summer.

By following Nature, that is, giving correct thought to appropriateness in the matter of

COLORS THAT MAY AND MAY NOT BE

Type of Woman	Black	White	Brown	Blue
Fair Blonde Hair—flaxen or golden. Eyes—blue, gray, or brown. Complexion—clear; little color.	Good; especially if of high luster and with touches of bright colors and white.	Good; especially clear or oyster white.	Good; especially very dark shades and green-brown, or bronze.	Good; all shades, if not too brilliant, including delft, turquoise, and peacock.
Titian Blonde Hair—red. Eyes—blue, gray, or brown. Complexion—medium clear and clear white; varying color.	Good; especially transparent black.	Good; especially cream and ivory.	Rich, deep, dark brown is all right. Avoid tans and yellow browns.	Good; especially blue-gray, midnight or darkest navy, and soft, silent tones.
Blonde-Brunette, or "In-Between" Type Hair—light chestnut or brown tone. Eyes—hazel, gray, blue-gray, or brown. Complexion—medium.	Fair; good if used with trimmings of color or white.	Good; especially clear white or with pink tint.	Fair; pinkish tan and golden brown best.	Good; intensifies the color of blue-gray eyes. Avoid very bright hues.
Pale Brunette Hair—black or dark brown. Eyes—brown, gray, or blue. Complexion—clear. Skin—fair; varying color.	Good, if white vest or collar is used or if delicate color of soft material is used as trimming.	Good; especially pure cream and ivory.	Fair; all shades.	Good; all shades. Electric and sapphire excellent if eyes are blue.
Olive Brunette Hair—dark brown or black. Eyes—clear brown or black. Complexion—dark in tone. Skin—smooth. Lips—very deep red, sometimes with a purplish tinge.	Avoid.	Excellent; especially ivory and cream.	Fair in very dark shades. Mahogany with cream for collar is excellent.	Excellent if very dark.
Florid Brunette Hair—black or dark brown. Eyes—black, brown, or gray. Complexion—dark. Skin—highly colored.	Very good; especially with color touches and yokes of cream or écru lace.	Good; especially cream and ivory.	Good; especially golden, tan, and nut browns.	Very pale, dark, or peacock, devoid of purple tinge, are best.
Sallow Mature Woman Hair—gray or white. Eyes—brown, blue, or gray. Complexion—sallow, without color.	Good only with white or cream and touch of bright color.	Only cream and milk white are good.	Avoid.	Midnight and navy, without any tinge of purple, are good.
Fair-Skinned Mature Woman Hair—gray or white Eyes—blue, brown, or gray. Complexion—fair; good coloring in lips and cheeks.	All right if relieved by white or palest écru collar, yoke, or vest.	Excellent.	Very dark, but not golden, brown is good; seal and chestnut are best.	Use only dull old blues, pastel tints, and midnight blue.

ORN BY DIFFERENT TYPES OF WOMEN

een	Gray	Purple	Red	Yellow	Pink
oth light rk.	Good; especially pearl, dove, and warm shades.	Good; especially heliotrope, wisteria, and blue-violet.	Dark and brilliant shades, like golf red, are best.	Avoid all except very pale yellow.	Good; all delicate or subdued shades, from lightest to old rose.
darkest of pure : and . Avoid reen unnplexion y clear lor good.	Good; especially gray with a pink cast.	Avoid. If complexion is clear and white, darkest and lightest lavender or violet may be used.	Avoid.	Fair. Dark, rich orange or amber tones are best as trimming, or veiled by white or black.	Lightest tints all right. Shell and flesh best.
specially een.	Clear or blue-gray fair. Avoid combinations of gray and black.	Fair; darkest shades are best. Very clear complexions may wear lavender.	Good in darkest shades, especially if used with very dark blue.	Palest yellow fair. Avoid écru tints.	Good; especially pale pink and rose
ie shades nze, re- nd bot- good.	Good; all shades, especially pearl, dove, blue-gray, and color gray.	Fair: must be used carefully. Orchid is good.	Only dark red, such as garnet and burgundy, is good.	Mustard, amber, and canary yellows are best.	Good; all pinks, except where cheeks are highly colored.
dark, ones.	Fair if warm color gray.	Use cautiously. Egg plant is permissible.	Excellent; especially the dark, warm shades.	Terra-cotta or fawn shades are good if cautiously used. Apricot in sheer material or as trimming is excellent.	Excellent in delicate tints. Salmon is especially good.
reen is	Silver gray is best.	Avoid. Not becoming.	Cardinal, crimson, and clear red are best.	Good; including any tone from orange to ivory.	Coral, rose (pale), old rose, and flesh are best.
	Good when of warm color gray.	Avoid, except in dull tones and with white at neck. Some lilac may be used.	Avoid, except in dull wine shades and with white at neck.	Avoid.	Only old rose is good.
hades ed the s black d.	Stone and lighter tones relieved by white at neck and brightened by a touch of color are all right.	Use only heliotrope (dull tone), grape, and darkest shade.	Avoid.	Use palest buff only.	Use palest and wild-rose shades only.

color and choosing gowns and wraps suitable for each season, there will be little chance for repetition of color in your wardrobe; likewise, there will be greater opportunity for you to work out a color scheme in gowns, wraps, hats, shoes, and accessories and thereby avoid the extravagances in dress so often accredited to women.

COLORS FOR VARIOUS TYPES

To aid you in the selection of color, I have introduced here a table that shows which colors may be worn successfully, as well as which colors should be avoided, by the eight recognized types of women: the fair blonde; the Titian, or red-haired, blonde; the blonde-brunette, or "in-between" type; the pale brunette; the olive brunette; the florid brunette; the sallow mature woman; and the fair-skinned mature woman.

In using this table you should keep in mind that a woman's age must always receive due consideration. Deep pink, for example, is usually for the youthful, while for the woman of sixty or more, white, delicate pink, flesh, rose, mulberry, black, dark blue, gray-blue, gray, and some shades of purple, such as lavender and pink-violet, are the most becoming

From youth to old age, every woman can wear white. Of course, not all women can wear pure, or blue, white, but then there are the milk, cream, and pink whites from which to select.

Also, it is well to know that all cold colors should be avoided by persons with sallow complexions; they should resort to warm colors and tones A person with a perfectly clear complexion, though, may wear any color that does not clash with the color of her hair.

The range of colors given in this table for Titian, or red-haired, blonde may with slight variations of shades and tints be safely followed in all the varying degrees of complexion.

Black for the pale-brunette type is always less trying if a cream-white vest or collar is used with it, or if some delicate color in soft material is employed as trimming. Brown is not good if the complexion is imperfect or inclined to noticeable sallowness or if the eyes lack the brilliancy characteristic of this type

The sallow mature woman is by far the most difficult type of woman to dress For this reason, great care should be exercised in the selection of every color given for this type in the table. Any color selected should be of the gray, shell, or pastel tone, rather than of brilliant quality. Bright colors introduced to given character or develop design should be used intelligently and very sparingly. Large splashes of color should never be used near the face, because this will not have the desired effect of brightening up the face, as is usually supposed, but will add to the sallowness of the complexion. Even white should be of the soft milk, cream, or pink tint, rather than a pure, or blue, white, which is as hard and brilliant as if it possessed color

The part of the table for the fair-skinned mature woman contains information for the prematurely gray-haired woman—that is, the woman whose hair is the only indication of approaching age and whose coloring and figure still retain their youthful qualities—and also for the mature woman who cannot be robbed of the brilliancy and beauty of complexion or youthful figure by age.

The prematurely gray may successfully wear materials of mixed color, such as two-tone fabrics in which the less vivid color predominates; that is, fabrics in which the more brilliant color is the underwoven color This type can wear rather brilliant colors also, provided they are veiled with transparent white, black, or dark colors of somber tone.

To broaden your knowledge of color, think not only of the colors for yourself, but also of colors appropriate for your friends This will increase your interest in color as well as in art, for color is a requisite of art, and a knowledge of art comes by study and application—comes to you only through conscious effort

ELSIE FERGUSON

Who knows clothes and how to make them carry the lines of dress to success for her as she herself carries the lines of the play

Artcraft Pictures

CHAPTER VI

BEAUTY IN LINES OF FIGURE AND DRESS

LINE THE INDICATOR OF GRACE—HOW TO EXPRESS LINES—THE CHARM OF LITHESOMENESS AND POISE—THE PROPER CORSET—CORRECT PROPORTIONS OF THE HUMAN FIGURE—OVERCOMING IRREGULARITIES—DRESS SUGGESTIONS FOR THE STOUT WOMAN.

Some women instinctively feel "line" and are graceful in consequence.

The artist feels and knows lines. The woman who designs, makes, and wears garments must know line and balance to be able to make garments that express individuality Women who are interested in dress in its highest sense realize that clothes to be effective must express the personality of the wearer.

Elsie Ferguson, one of America's most attractive women, delightfully expresses her individuality in her clothes. The long, graceful lines that she effects give grace and dignity to every movement of her body To see Elsie Ferguson on the stage, to forget the theme of the play, and to study the lines of her costumes will give sufficient evidence of the value of lines. Indeed, such a study will convince any woman that she can make herself more attractive if she learns to know the lines that are best suited to her type.

The woman who makes a career for herself on the stage studies herself—her expression and her movements—learns her good and bad points, and as a result invariably gives more consideration to the lines of her costume, to the gracefulness of her body, than she does to her face and coiffure.

Every woman should realize her possibilities and make the most of them. Study and observation, with determination, will make it possible to achieve much in the way of improvement Dinner parties, receptions, all manner of things are given on the stage, and every person there represents a certain type of character and has his or her part in making the scene beautiful When planning to go to a dinner, a party, or a reception, plan to make yourself a decorative part of the surroundings, to dress yourself in such a way that you will add to the attractiveness of the assemblage, so that you will make a pleasing picture, rather than the one jarring note.

Emily Burbank, in her book on "Woman as Decoration," writes at great length upon the value of woman as decoration. She gives chapters about how a woman should decorate her garden, her drawing room, her boudoir, by dressing appropriately and being beautiful in it, by dressing herself to be the most beautiful thing in her living room or at her dinner table.

The wonderful art galleries of the world and the histories of all times tell us that women have been and are the most decorative of all created things. They have supplied the inspiration for the most wonderful paintings, for the most beautiful pieces of statuary, for decorations on vases, and even for the designs on our moneys, all because they are to the artist the source of his loftiest inspiration.

What has the artist portrayed in the beautiful picture on canvas or vase? Not the face alone, but the lines of the figure, the lines of the gown, the drapery of the gown, most often, and the great artists find woman most graceful in gowns that hang from the shoulder; but even such gowns may be so modernized as to fit in the social life or the office of today and be entirely appropriate and far more beautiful than a gown that is cut up in small pieces and put together in patchwork fashion.

HOW TO EXPRESS LINES

Harmonious lines in dress require correct carriage of the body to express them. A knowledge of the lines of face and figure is essential to the successful adaptation of lines in dress A knowledge of stature and correct posture is necessary if any degree of personality or individuality is to be emphasized. To stand correctly is the first requisite of a graceful figure In the beauty of correct posture lies much of the charm of many of the celebrated pieces of sculpture, such as the martial "Winged Victory" and the beautiful "Venus of Milo."

Dr. Walter L. Pyle, in his book on "Personal Hygiene" tells in a few words how to stand correctly. His rule is exactly what every woman should daily apply to herself:

> The erect standing posture is maintained by holding the body as tall as possible without actually rising on to the toes. In this way the trunk (your body) is given its greatest length; there is the largest space available for the organs; the muscles of the front, back, and sides are in perfect balance, none are strained; the head is erect and so poised that none of the muscles are overworked.

Apply this rule to yourself; practice standing just as tall as you can without throwing your weight on your toes. Every time you are standing, think of it and practice it. In one week's time, you will see improvement; in six weeks, you will wonder how you ever stood in an incorrect way, for correct posture rests you, it is better for you physically, and makes you much more attractive; besides, your clothes will appear fifty per cent. better when you stand erect in them.

Books and books have been written on correct posture. One author goes so far as to say that any woman can be beautiful if she acquires a correct carriage, because it is her figure that attracts the greatest amount of attention. We American women are accredited with giving little thought to how we stand, it being said of us that our posture is ugly, that we stand with one hip down, just as a horse does when it is tired or asleep. We do it—you do and so do I. But we know it is not a pleasing sight for our friends When people whom we respect come into our presence, we immediately stand erect and make ourselves "as tall as possible."

Why not practice persistently standing correctly for six weeks and let it become a habit (habits, you know, can be formed for good as well as for bad), so that we will always stand properly and not have to gather ourselves together as if picking up a lapful of sewing upon the approach of our friends?

"Pep" in your step. What has that to do with the attractiveness of woman?

The most graceful woman I ever knew was extremely light on her feet. Though weighing at least one hundred and fifty pounds, she moved about lightly, quickly, deftly. To be graceful, you must be light on your feet. This is not hard to do. Practice lifting the body up and walking quickly, and avoid planting your full weight on your feet with each step. Thoughtful watching will enable you to acquire this desirable habit.

It has been said that a man who wears a soldier's uniform for any length of time can always be recognized when in civilian clothes because of the erectness of his body and his correct posture, whether sitting or standing. It is noticeable around military camps, where soldiers are drilling and practicing, that both men and women who live near and see them hold up their shoulders and walk more correctly than do persons who are not in close contact with the military atmosphere.

I remember quite well of having been sitting in a railway station in a big city, observing the people as they passed to and fro. I saw a number of soldiers in uniform, and noticed that they walked with so much more assurance and confidence than the civilians that I wished every man could wear the uniform a little while just for the purpose of making him appreciate the benefits to be derived from standing correctly.

At this same time, I noticed a group of sitting, waiting women. I am sorry to say the picture they made was not pleasing. They were crumpled up as though friendless, ambitionless, and spiritless, sitting with their heads down, their backs looking long, draggly, and tired The effect of seeing these people made me want to sit up straight to throw off any appearance of fatigue; in fact, this was necessary in order to overcome the mental depression that these pictures caused.

The devotee of the one-time popular "débutante slouch" is looked upon as lazy or semi-ill, rather than blasé or aristocratic.

THE CHARM OF LITHESOMENESS AND POISE

Sarah Bernhardt, the great dramatic artist, says of women: "Prettiness does not matter. If a woman has charm and energy, she can secure whatever else she desires—love, success, power."

At this point, I want to make a clear distinction between prettiness and beauty. The woman who has a highly powdered, rouged face, with fluffy, frizzled hair, may be pretty;

but the woman who is wholesome, clean, neat, and charming is beautiful—yes beautiful even after a whole day's picnicking or shopping or working.

The pretty woman, if constantly within range of powder puff and mirror, may retain her prettiness, but I would encourage you to acquire beauty and then judiciously apply prettiness, and, as your reward, be attractive, distinctive, and—a beautiful woman.

The plainest woman can be wholesome, can express lithesomeness, vitality, charm, and can dress becomingly—a combination that will make her so attractive that she will unquestionably appear pleasing.

Lithesome! Isn't that a fascinating word? Almost as much so as *happiness* No; really not so fascinating. Happiness says so much, means so much, is so much to be desired and so precious to possess that none, not even the poorest of us, would sell it for great wealth! Happiness radiates beauty—that elusive, exquisite quality we all persistently seek to express

But, to get back to the word lithesome. I like to think of it in connection with woman.

Lithesomeness challenges age, for it gives a youthful step and grace in movement, and shows that you are master of your body.

Lithesomeness helps to accentuate poise, too, for it expresses freedom, the abandonment of restraint. And poise expresses what? Mental strength, for poise comes only to those whose minds have supreme power over their faculties.

Lithesomeness and poise—two delightful qualities. When you possess both, your friends will pronounce you charming.

If you possess a spirit of happiness, you may acquire lithesomeness through bodily exercise that is systematic and persistent. And poise, too, may be cultivated, for it comes through study, continuous efforts toward self-improvement, and the daily, yes, hourly, practicing of the Golden Rule.

So much is said about the importance, the necessity, of physical exercise that I am sure you realize its value, the necessity of exercising every day.

In days gone by, women of leisure did not exercise. They, as a rule, became fat at forty, and at forty-five they were old women. Few lived past the age of forty-five. Why? Because they wore ugly, tight corsets that gave no freedom and they were so frail, so delicate, that when illness assailed them they were as susceptible to it as a drunkard is to pneumonia and as incurable.

Now, however, the woman of leisure has charities, work for her country, has swimming, golf, motoring—all manner of work and sport to give exercise. The woman who keeps her own home has some of these, too, for cleaning, sweeping, dusting, bedmaking—all tend to give her a lithesome, graceful body.

The office girl usually has access to a gymnasium or a bathing pool. If she has not, she can easily secure a chart or a book written by a reputable teacher of physical culture and study and practice hygiene, as well as helpful exercises that will keep her body young and keep away any evidence of superfluous flesh

THE PROPER CORSET

Corsets have much to do with the appearance of women who wear them and also with their comfort and discomfort and, consequently, their disposition, for it can be truly said that corsets that fit properly are the next thing to a blessing, whereas ill-fitting corsets can provide as much food for ill temper as can any other one thing.

That a knowledge of how to proceed in the selection of corsets is a valuable asset for any woman will not be denied The accuracy and care with which the dresses of today are designed and made absolutely demand correct-fitting corsets No one can afford to build a garment or a costume smart and stylish to the last detail and then have all its distinctiveness lost or its lines distorted by wearing it over a corset that does not fit properly.

In buying corsets you will do well to consult the sales person of the corset shop or of the corset department of a store regarding the kind of corset that is best for your build; yet you should know yourself the kind of corset that you can wear with the greatest comfort and, also, the kind that gives you the very best lines

It is reasonable to believe that any woman will select corsets with care if she knows how to proceed.

Some manufacturers claim that there are nine types of women to be fitted with corsets, and all up-to-date corset makers provide corsets for these types. They are: (1) The short, slender figure; (2) the tall, slender figure; (3) the short-waisted figure; (4) the short, heavy figure; (5) the tall, heavy figure; (6) the full-hip figure; (7) the full-bust figure; (8) the swayed-back figure; and (9) the perfect figure

In the following table I am giving a brief outline of the kinds of corsets to be worn by these various types of figure:

Type of Figure	Kind of Corset
Short, slender figure	Moderately short, light in weight, with few stays; never tight.
Tall, slender figure..	Light in weight, with few stays, but long enough over hips to give an unbroken line.
Short-waisted figure	. Corset short below waist-line in front. Should be fitted loose and pulled down well on figure.
Short, heavy figure.	Corset with short stays, to avoid pushing up when wearer sits, thus making her appear short-waisted.
Tall, heavy figure..	Corset with very long skirt. Must be short in front, however, length coming at back and sides.
Full-hip figure .	..Corset short-waisted, long and closely boned over the hips. Several elastics to be fastened to hose to avoid break at bottom of corset
Full-bust figure	Corset loose enough above waist-line to allow flesh to fall into corset and thus make it less prominent; or, low-busted corset may be worn and flesh confined in tight-fitting brassière.
Swayed-back figure	. Ordinary corset, but if back is very much curved and if figure is especially flat below the waist-line a small corset pad attached to inside of corset where needed. (Pad may be made of three or more thicknesses of sheet wadding covered with China silk.)
Perfect figure	Correct size for waist and of comfortable length and weight.

As a general rule, the size of corset should be two to four inches smaller than the original waist measurement, but the large woman should not buy her corset to fit her waist measurement, as the size of her hips will have much to do with the size of her corset The large woman should guard against wearing too small a corset.

A corset should never be worn too tight, for this makes the slender woman appear more slender, and it is apt to make the large woman appear to be "all corsets" A corset worn tight above the waist pushes the bust up and makes it appear still larger, while if tight over the hips the line at the termination of the corset will show, and this gives a very ugly appearance.

CORRECT PROPORTIONS OF THE HUMAN FIGURE

Perhaps you have never realized it, but it is true that the lines of your figure have as great a bearing upon what you may wear becomingly as color has. Indeed, if you wish to utilize to the best advantage the ideas presented from day to day by fashion authorities, you must have a knowledge of the lines of the human form.

To come to such a knowledge and thereby appreciate the value of lines in dress and adapt them to your figure, it is absolutely essential to have a clear understanding of the correct proportions of the parts of the human figure. Thus, the relative proportion of the head and and the body as to length and width, the proportion of the waist length to the skirt length, the length of the arm as compared to the length of the waist, the position of the head on the shoulders, the width of the shoulders and the chest in proportion to the width of the back, the size and height of the neck in proportion to the length of the front and the width of the chest—all these and other factors govern the design of harmonious garments, because a clear comprehension of them makes it possible to plan and construct garments that will overcome defects and irregularities and yet be very attractive.

So that you may form a definite idea of what your proportions must be in order to be considered as an evenly proportioned figure, I have tabulated the dimensions. In stating such proportions, the custom is to designate the measurements in so many heads, the term *head* meaning the distance from the bottom of the chin to the top of the forehead. Of course, persons of different sizes have heads of different sizes; therefore, your head governs your own measurements or proportions.

	Heads
Height, from top of head to the floor.. .	8
From tip of chin to bottom of breastbone..	1
From bottom of breastbone to waist line .	$\frac{3}{4}$
Under arm, from armhole to waist line ..	1
Arm, or armhole measure....... .. .	2
Bust, which usually is two inches smaller than hip measurement..	$4\frac{1}{4}$
From top of forehead to waist line.......	$2\frac{3}{4}$
Width of hip, from side to side	2
Thickness of hips..	$1\frac{1}{6}$
Hip measurement	$4\frac{1}{2}$
Waist-line measurement	3
From waist line to fullest part or dart point, or beginning of legs............	1
From beginning of legs to bottom of knee..	$2\frac{1}{4}$
From bottom of knee to the floor. . ..	2
Length of skirt from waist line to the floor	$5\frac{1}{4}$

Although the correct height of an evenly proportioned woman is eight heads, as is mentioned in the list, artists in making drawings of figures, as well as in rendering pictorial designs of styles, generally choose a height of ten heads. This is done so as to bring out perfection in appearance, for it is true that actual photographs of perfect figures, even if the models are very slender, always appear short and thick

This information will help you to follow intelligently the designs in fashion magazines that attempt to overcome, by use of artistic drawings, the squatty appearance a photograph gives the really perfect figure.

In connection with the measurements given, it may be well also to state that if the distance from the top of the forehead to the waist line is less than two and three-fourth heads, you would be considered short-waisted; and of course, the reverse is true—a distance greater than two and three-fourth heads would mean that you are long-waisted.

OVERCOMING IRREGULARITIES

It is frequently asked, "How can a woman who has apparently no intuition or instinctive sense of line really come to know line and its relation to her and to her clothes?"

Line, as it is used in connection with the lines of the human figure and in connection with dress, requires, first, a knowledge of the proportions of the human figure; then, a careful and truthful self-analysis.

You should study the table of measurements, determine for yourself whether or not you are long-waisted, short-waisted, broad for your height, or slender for your height, and then make an earnest effort in selecting your clothes to conceal any irregularity in proportion.

Notice every dress you see, whether it is worn in the street, in the home, on a fashion manikin, or illustrated in women's magazines, fashion books, or your daily newspaper. Associate the lines of the dress with your figure and the figures that you know, and constantly reason with yourself what you would use, why you would use it, what you would avoid, and why you would avoid it.

You may be well proportioned and have a very beautiful figure even if your measurements do not coincide with those I have given. Still, if you do not measure up correctly, you should strive, in garment planning and construction, to secure a correct balance and in this way attract as little attention as possible to any irregularity in figure

For example, if your shoulders are narrower than your hips and your figure is not too stout, make your waists and blouses with long shoulder effects, berthas, and frills, or with plaits and tucks of a style that will give the impression of width through the shoulders; likewise, cut your skirts with straight lines or lines that will give length, in order to make the hips appear smaller.

If your waist is short in proportion to your skirt length, select designs and color combinations that do not tend to accentuate this irregularity. A very common mistake in such cases is to wear a high-waist-line skirt or a dark belt with a white or a light-colored shirtwaist. If you are of this type, choose only skirts with regulation waist lines and wear light belts that match the waist in color, or, better still, wear a belt that is part of the waist or the blouse.

If your hips are high and heavy, wear skirts that tend to equalize the figure below the hip line; also, carry trimming lines low, and in this way draw the eye of the observer away from the prominent lines.

The short-waisted woman is usually of generous proportions, with a full, high bust If this means you, pay attention to your corsets and the lines of your dress or waist. Wear a corset that has a medium bust height and plenty of room for the bust and shoulder fulness to drop naturally, especially when sitting, and confine this part of the figure in a good-fitting brassière, one that is not tight at its lower edge. Likewise, avoid yoke lines or contrasting color trimming lines that tend to cut the figure in two, and use instead long, slightly pointed lines to carry the eye down rather than around the figure. In dresses that will permit it, these lines should be extended down the skirt length, for it gives the appearance of greater height and slimness.

If you happen to be a high-hip figure, avoid short-yoke effects. You will always look well in skirts with plaited fulness just below the hip line.

If your skirt length is short in proportion to your waist length, locate the waist line of your dresses so that it will bring about a well-balanced figure.

Things that the short-waisted figure should avoid can be successfully used by the short-skirt figure The length of the bodice if it is worn over the skirt, the height of the waist line of the skirt itself, or the position of the girdle or the belt may be adjusted to give the effect of a long or a short waist or skirt, as the proportion of the figure demands

If you are a short woman, lines that run across, either for trimmings or on skirts, are not for you any more than they are for a woman whose body is long in proportion to her legs. Such lines, however, are a boon to the tall woman, as well as to the woman whose legs are long in proportion to her body, to the woman who should not wear striped materials made in up-and-down effect or long, unbroken skirt lengths

If your arms are long, you can wear trimmed or double sleeves well, provided their lines do not come at a point where they may create an ugly appearance because of a low, full bust or high hips.

If your arms are shorter than the average, you should avoid such sleeves, no matter what the style may be at the time. The sleeves must come to just the right point on the arm to be correct. They may come to the wrist, to a point just a short distance above the wrist, or to the point where the curve of the lower arm joins the elbow; they should never come just to the elbow, but they may come just above the elbow where the curve of the upper arm begins; also, they may come at the termination of the muscle on the upper arm near the top of the shoulder or just far enough over the top of the shoulder to show the curved turn of the shoulder.

Because of the American woman's characteristically short neck, which, if not a prominent feature in youth, develops as she takes on flesh, it is wise for nearly every woman to think twice before wearing a high standing collar. A collar shaped to roll a little high at the back and to slope to a graceful line in front is usually much better, and it may adhere as closely as is necessary to any fashion requirement.

A low neck line to be really pretty and correct should slope lower to the front than to the back; indeed, if this rule is not followed, the figure is usually displeasing.

This rule applies to yoke lines also, but it does not carry the same weight when making a décolleté gown. Then the back neck line may be considerably lower, but it is best to have this line of different shape; for instance, if a round front line is used, the back neck line should be V- or U-shaped

The height of the bust line should always be taken into account in connection with the neck line. If your neck is large, the bust should be kept as low as possible in order to give a good length and thus make the neck appear smaller than it is. When square necks are worn, they should be carefully proportioned to the width of the chest and the length of the front.

Flesh at the back of the neck, just below the neck line, is almost as noticeable as a goiter, even if it is not so prominent, for the chin overshadows to some extent the goiter at the front of the neck line, whereas the flesh at the back is very prominent, particularly if the hair is done up high on the head.

Many women are sensitive about this, and persist in wearing high collars to conceal it; others are of the opinion that the collar accentuates the flesh, and wear dresses that are low at the back of the neck The latter plan is unsatisfactory, however, as the flesh will show very prominently from the side. A better way is to have the neck line extended about half way over the fleshy portion and thus make it less prominent.

A good rule to follow in overcoming all such irregularities as a full bust, extremely high or low hips, a large waist, and so on, is this: Do not overtrim or accentuate prominent figure features by the application of buttons, braids, frogs, embroidery, or any other trimming; instead, employ trimming details so as to detract from such features

In giving instructions to classes of young women interested in knowing dress in its highest sense, I have frequently found it helpful to suggest that they dress up their friends, and you may do the same with profit Take some member of your own family, for instance, your mother, and design for her a dress that expresses her motherliness—her type Then, choose a color that will help make her hair appear the softest and her eyes the kindliest.

Try this You will find it easy to think of the color and to plan the fabric, for, usually, the material most suitable for one's mother has a smooth surface, is soft in texture, and is subdued in color.

When you begin to consider her figure, you may find that the bust and hips are large in proportion to the height, that the hips are large in proportion to the bust, or that the back length is long in proportion to the front length Then you have a problem of lines

For many years, mothers who have acquired a little more flesh than is becoming have found it difficult to procure appropriate clothes. It is not uncommon to see a woman who is overweight wearing a corset entirely too tight and much too high above the waist line, and a dress fitted as closely as possible around the waist, thus emphasizing the ugliest feature of the overweight figure.

Manufacturers of stout women's apparel have frequently said: "Camouflage the stout woman"; that is, get materials that have large figures and indistinct colorings in patches so that the silhouette of the body will not be in evidence and that the optic nerve will not be able to conceive how large the figure actually is.

But few would like to camouflage their mothers as regards dress They would rather have a dress simple in color and design and plan it to hang from the shoulder—a dress that has a soft belt coming around in a way that will give length to the waist line and not tell every one precisely within one-fourth inch where the waist line begins and where it ends

One girl who tried this method of learning lines designed some dresses for her mother, who weighed nearly one hundred and eighty pounds and was only five feet three inches in height

One of the most successful dresses that she made was of silk, a maroon-and-taupe stripe. The stripes were irregular, and there were two maroon stripes to every one of taupe. The dress was made in Russian-blouse effect, with a simple straight skirt, the Russian blouse coming almost to the knees. A long collar of flesh-color crêpe was used for the front, coming down in a V. The sleeves were close-fitting, with a little plain cuff of crêpe The waist line was finished with a belt, the stripes encircling the waist, a maroon stripe in the center and a taupe one on each side. The belt, which was narrow, crossed in the back and looped at the left side front It went around the figure twice—at the normal waist line and below it—and thus gave length to the waist line Its crossing in the back took away the severe plainness of the back, and yet did not interfere with the length.

The plain, straight sleeves did not emphasize the heaviness in the arms, and the crêpe collar gave just enough coloring to the face. The line of the collar gave a long neck line, which helped to avoid emphasizing the roundness of the face.

When this woman sat down in this costume, it was graceful and comfortable. The lower skirt fell gracefully down to her ankles, making it much more pleasing than if she had had a tight skirt that would draw up around her figure. This girl—this designer—knew that a dress should be as beautiful when the wearer is sitting as when she is standing.

So becoming was this dress for the mother that the daughter made some house dresses of chambray, gray-and-white stripe for one and blue-and-white for another. But she clung almost slavishly to this one design of dress. She gave as her reason, "I know it is best."

She did not cling to stripes, however, because I once saw her mother wearing a very dark-blue silk that was just as pretty as the stripes, but the lines of the dress were almost identical with the one I had seen made of the striped material.

DRESS SUGGESTIONS FOR THE STOUT WOMAN

In discussing in this book ways in which to overcome irregularities of the figure, I would fall short of my wish to be "helpful to all women" if I made no suggestions that pertain directly to the stout woman.

True it is that the stout woman has greater odds to overcome than her thin sister and her sister of medium form, for it would seem that they can wear anything and everything devised by fashion authorities; yet there is no reason why the stout woman should become disheartened, for she can and must adopt ideas that will be to her advantage

As a general rule, a woman does not become noticeably stout until she has reached the neighborhood of forty This time of life is usually the most trying for any woman, for when youth is on the wing it makes necessary three things if a woman is to continue to appear attractive and pleasing.

The first of these three things is dignity, the second careful grooming, and the third a correct selection of color, lines, and fabric, together with correct corseting. These three things are necessary if a woman's entire costume is to be in perfect harmony with her individuality, quietly suggesting absolute comfort and ease

The saying, "Nobody loves a fat man," may be applied to the stout woman, too, for it is equally true that nobody admires a fat woman —that is, if she *looks* fat

To avoid looking fat, the fleshy woman must constantly be a law unto herself If you belong to this class, you should not adopt all the fads and fancies that come into fashion's realm each season; rather, you must be entirely independent and use good judgment regarding every part of your costume For instance, if your neck is short and thick, you should not wear "choker" collars of any kind, no matter what fashion dictators say. You should wear about the neck soft lace that may be brought down in front in a V neck line, which is a boon to the person with a short neck, and if lace is used to finish the neck it should be of a quality and texture that will blend in with the waist or bodice and seemingly be lost to the eye.

Many stout women complain that the styles are made for the slender woman and that no thought is given to them. This, however, is untrue, for fashion people, as a rule, knowing the difficulties encountered by many women who possess an abundance of flesh, really do give a great deal of attention to designing attractive garments for them.

To get the best results, the woman of this type should realize that a garment made for her should not be an exact copy of the prevailing fashion, but rather an adaptation of that style to suit her proportions and give individual line.

Two things should always be borne in mind by the stout woman in choosing a garment; namely, that up-and-down lines give slenderness and round-and-round lines tend to accentuate thickness.

The waists that may be worn advantageously by the stout woman are those with straight vests and "Gibson plaits," those with yokes formed of tucks that are straight from the shoulder down, surplice waists, and, in fact, any waist with lines that extend lengthwise of the figure.

Skirts, whether full or narrow, that are cut as long as possible without attracting undue attention to their length or causing discomfort, long tunic skirts, plain, straight-plaited skirts, and panels are desirable for the stout woman; but she should avoid tiered skirts or skirts with ruffles, shirring, and excessive or crosswise trimming.

The sleeves for the stout woman should be plain and soft in appearance and have a tendency to cling to the arm If the forearm is large and heavy, a sleeve that comes just below the elbow or at a point three or four inches above the wrist is suitable.

Long, bulky sleeves, however, should never be worn on a heavy forearm. If long sleeves are worn, they should be made to fit very close below the elbow, and the lower part of the sleeve should be finished with a frill of lace or fabric or with a moderately small, light-weight, flaring cuff, which will make the hand appear smaller when a glove is not worn.

The stout woman should never expose her shoulders and upper arms when in evening attire; rather, she should cover the flesh with filmy lace or chiffon, or she should wear a scarf of tulle, preferably of black or silent tone, across the shoulders and the arms White will make the arms appear larger than they are, and black will give the opposite effect.

In trimming garments, the stout woman should remember that buttons or trimmings placed in flat patch effect, as in squares, triangles, or diamonds, will tend to add thickness, while if they are arranged in single rows or broken lines they will give the appearance of length instead of breadth.

Use should always be made of trimmings in harmonizing, rather than contrasting, colors, so that they will not stand out boldly from the garment.

Never should the collar, the belt, or the finish at the bottom of the skirt be permitted to attract the eye before the garment itself does. Instead, they should be arranged so as to be as inconspicuous as possible, and in using tucks, plaits, or seams they should be made to extend up and down the garment instead of around it.

In selecting material for garments, the stout woman frequently makes the mistake of choosing wide stripes, having perhaps heard or read that stripes tend to make a person look slender. She can wear striped material, but the stripes, as a rule, must be fine and without define color or line.

Stout women, and, in fact, most women, look better in materials of plain or indistinct design in harmonizing colors than in decided color combinations.

It is always well to remember, too, that materials with glossy, brilliant surface or finish, no matter what the color of the fabric may be, are difficult to wear and are not generally becoming, because the sheen and in some instances the stiffness of the fabric tend to make the figure appear larger; whereas, materials of soft finish or dull colors will make the figure appear smaller and attract less attention.

In selecting material for skirts, stout women should usually choose plain fabric with a narrow or an invisible stripe and of a texture that is as soft and pliable as Dame Fashion permits.

BILLIE BURKE

Simplicity dignifies her costumes and helps her to radiate the delightful charm of womanhood

Famous Players

CHAPTER VII

IMPORTANCE OF SUITABLE FABRICS

RELATION OF COLOR, LINE, AND FABRIC—SUCCESSFUL COMBINING OF FABRICS—SUITABILITY OF FABRIC DESIGNS FOR INDIVIDUALS—GUARDING AGAINST CONTRADICTORY LINES—SUITABILITY OF FABRICS.

Having told you about color and line, I must next direct your attention to the importance of fabric in distinctive dress. It is on three things—color, line, and fabric—that dress harmony depends

A prominent textile manufacturer said to me one time, repeating his statement twice, with emphasis, "Women must learn to appreciate textiles in order to use them properly."

In further conversation, I found that he held considerable sentiment regarding the using of fabrics for certain purposes. He seemed to know just how, where, and by whom velvet, charmeuse, voile, organdie, gingham, and all other fabrics should be worn

We frequently err—miserably err—in our use of fabrics, and this is a pity. If we realized the important part that fabrics play in supplying our needs, in helping us to express individuality in dress, we would study them and respect them

The textile industry is of great importance, being the third largest industry in the world Hundreds and hundreds of people of artistic ability lend their energies toward making beautiful fabrics, and the woman who knows how much skill and effort are put into the creating of one yard of silk, of one yard of wool, or of a bit of lace cannot handle a piece of material without experiencing a certain amount of reverence and respect. When she has this feeling or attitude toward materials, she will almost intuitively know how to use them properly.

Fabric and its color may be said to control the lines and the purpose of a garment, for, as you will readily see, the design of a garment depends considerably on the weight of the fabric and its colors.

To illustrate my point, let us take a fluffy, airy fabric Such fabric at once suggests a design of frills and puffs Such a design, in turn, controls the garment lines, because frills and puffs in nowise conform to the silhouette of the figure. Also, if such fabric is of a light shade or a brilliant hue, it will bring to mind a garment for evening wear, as such colors appear bright in artificial light. If it is white, or of a dark or subdued shade, it may suggest a dress for morning or afternoon wear.

Again, lines that conform to the silhouette of one's figure are suggested by tailoring fabrics or materials, because the weight of such fabrics will not bear development in either full or pretentious styles, it being necessary to press them firm and flat to bring out their real beauty.

SUCCESSFUL COMBINING OF FABRICS

In connection with fabrics, bear in mind that the material for a garment should always be suitable for the design that is to be used. Very frequently the mistake is made of trying to combine lace, frills, ruffles, and ribbon with materials suitable for only plain tailored designs or of trying to combine them into a fluffy style.

Just as garments of taffeta and other similar fabrics, lace, and so on should be as fluffy and feminine as it is possible to make them, so should tailoring materials be made into tailored gowns or suits that are as plain in line as prevailing styles will permit.

Do not attempt to use material with a hard surface in a design that has a tendency to stand out from the body The very fact that its surface is hard, wiry, and uncontrollable should be sufficient warning to employ it in only such a way as will give the most pleasing effect.

In using such contrary fabrics, pay attention to the color, too. Brilliant, hard colors should be avoided to get the best results. In such fabric, the softer the tone the softer will appear the garment when worn On the other hand, brighter colors may be used in crêpe de Chine and soft satins and taffetas, as these materials have a tendency to cling to the figure and thus give a softness of line that modifies the color

In draped designs, as in a skirt of several tiers, for instance, you can readily see how soft taffeta may be worked in artistically, each tier holding itself in its place and giving a very desirable effect.

So also may lace and other materials of soft, firm weave be used; but if you attempt to use in the same design a firm, hard material, such as brilliantine, alpaca, or mohair, all of which are of a seemingly contrary weave, the result will be disappointing, and especially will this be so if you employ such materials for ruffles, unlined boleros, berthas, shirring, and so on

Avoid using too many kinds of material in one dress; as, for instance, velvet, taffeta, and charmeuse. Do not use silk and cotton or cotton and linen together, unless you are positive that the combination is agreeable.

Velvet, because it is silk and because of its sheen, is better to use with satin, with its sheen, or with Georgette crêpe, which has absolutely no sheen and is soft and limp enough to give way entirely to the prominence of the velvet.

When heavy deep-colored material is used for the body of a dress, and sheerer sleeves are to be used, do not make the mistake of having the sleeve material too thin, as, for instance, to use chiffon instead of a fairly heavy quality of Georgette crêpe.

Avoid using silk voile and Georgette; satin and taffeta; serge and cheviot These materials "war" when in combination.

Do not use ribbon for a sash or a collar trimming on a dress that has satin or silk as a trimming, unless you use it cleverly and for a definite purpose Select material for collars with care A safe plan is to decide whether the purpose of the collar is to give a "light reflection" to the face, to soften the neck line, or to serve as a trimming feature Find your reason; then you will invariably use the correct material.

SUITABILITY OF FABRIC DESIGNS FOR INDIVIDUALS

For the sake of harmony, always give careful consideration to the design of a fabric. Large-figured materials, especially brocades, striped and plaid materials with prominent patterns, demand the greatest attention, because they are possibly the hardest of all materials to develop successfully.

A little girl can wear prominent plaids very well, because the lines of her garments are usually straight and simple and not cut up or broken; but she cannot wear large-figured brocades, because the body pieces of her garment are so small that the result would be patchy.

The large woman, however, can wear large-figured brocades very successfully, provided the lines of her garment are straight and plain and conform almost exactly to the outline of her figure; but the small woman, the same as the child, should avoid such materials, for she will not appear to the best advantage in them

The statement I have just made may appear contrary to the general rule, for it would seem that large-figured materials have a tendency to make small women appear larger; however, as such materials are most beautiful when developed in plain style, the brocade figures on a small woman might appear so prominent that the effect would not be pleasing.

In pompadour silks, however, the opposite is true. Taffetas with large bouquets of flowers are more attractive for the small woman, provided they are made in a fluffy fashion or if they are puffed in such a way, as in a pannier skirt, as not to appear broken or crushed; yet you should always remember that the heavy brocades, unless of taffeta, should be made up in straight lines, with the design as unbroken as possible.

One finds in the shops such a delightful variety of materials that there is no excuse for using any of them incorrectly.

A young girl of sixteen or eighteen is charming in ruffled and frilled organdie, provided her body is small enough to permit her to wear fluffy attire; but the woman of thirty-five or forty usually appears better in softer materials, such as voile and soft crêpes, because she should express dignity, because the lines in her face—and there are usually a few indistinct ones at that time—should be secluded and protected behind a background of friendly material

Hard-surface materials, such as cheviots and tweeds, are rarely becoming for a mature woman, because the softer smooth-surface materials, such as broadcloth and duvetyn, lend themselves so much better to her requirements.

The women of England exercise discrimination in wearing materials. In the morning, while shopping or on an outing expedition, they will be in tweeds or in plain, severely tailored materials. In the afternoon, they will be in soft velvets and broadcloth; in the evening, in velvets, silks, or soft crêpes, chiffons, and voiles, the material entirely in accord with the season and the fashion. These women have an inborn taste for the use of fabrics that many of us may well strive to acquire.

GUARDING AGAINST CONTRADICTORY LINES

To get proper results in dress designing, always guard very carefully against the use of contradictory lines—and by these I mean lines that do not run in the same direction; for instance, a round, square, or pointed yoke with belt or sleeve trimming used in an opposite way.

Such designs can be used harmoniously in one garment, provided great care is taken to keep the garment well balanced. However, if stripes are used in the yoke, belt, or cuffs, then the remaining stripes of the garment should, in nearly every case, run lengthwise in order to make part of the figure appear as trimming and the other as the body part of the garment.

Sometimes a pleasing effect may be had in one garment by arranging the stripes so as to be vertical, horizontal, and diagonal; but in most cases the effect is not pleasing, for it is without doubt a difficult style to develop successfully and only the most courageous would attempt to construct a garment in this way.

When plaids and stripes are used together, you will find that it is practically impossible to get a harmonious effect from them, because one detracts from the other, producing a very inharmonious result.

On the other hand, plain material combines admirably with either stripes or plaids, as it has a tendency to modify and yet give the desired prominence to the stripes or the plaid.

Large-figured brocades, pompadour silks, etc. are best made entirely of themselves; however, if lace or trimming is used with such materials, it should be less conspicuous than the material itself in order that the material may stand out and thus emphasize its own beauty.

Speaking of plaids and stripes brings to my mind a woman rather large in stature who dresses her hair very plain and wears plaid ginghams of vivid colorings in her home. She seems to have an endless number of such dresses, but they are so out of keeping with her surroundings as to jar your "respect for fabrics."

Plaids are beautiful. There is nothing really prettier for children than plaid ginghams; but they are rarely suitable for a woman whose very size demands no emphasis.

SUITABILITY OF FABRICS

There is a wealth of beauty in fabrics and they offer an excellent opportunity to express individuality and good taste in dress for the house, where so many people seem to think "it does not matter what you wear, so long as you are home." The simplest materials, such as the inexpensive cottons—voile, crêpe, chintz, and zephyr gingham—lend themselves delightfully to home dresses.

I know a woman whose first-floor rooms are very artistically furnished in blue and gray, whose boudoir is in rose and ivory, and whose sewing room—"her workshop" she calls it—is in softest gray. This woman, with this attractive, agreeable home, finds it necessary to do a great deal of the work of keeping it up herself.

In the morning, she will come down with a little dress of unbleached, unstarched, smoothly ironed muslin It may have a little cross-stitching of blue or a little soft lace collar, but it is so simple that it does not interfere with the surroundings, and no matter whether she is in the living room, in the dining room, or in the kitchen, she makes a pleasing picture.

In the afternoon, she may be in a little rose-colored or cream dress of soft voile, or it may be white, or it may be a light pink; but it is of a color sufficiently indefinite and of fabric soft enough not to conflict with the tints and shades and soft drapery effects in her rooms.

I like to let my eyes follow this woman around about in her home—see how the color and fabrics used in her frocks lend themselves to the furnishings of each and every room—how she seems to blend intimately and gracefully into the attractive background she has so cleverly provided.

CHAPTER VIII

DEVELOPING YOUR STYLE

GOOD TASTE IN DRESS—GETTING IDEAS FROM GOOD AND BAD DRESSERS—READY-TO-WEAR GARMENTS AS AN AID—HINTS FROM FASHION MAGAZINES—COLOR SUGGESTIONS FROM FASHION PLATES—INTERPRETING FASHIONS—OTHER SOURCES OF INFORMATION—ACQUIRING SUCCESSFUL RESULTS—YOUR STYLE.

When you have learned what type of garment is most becoming to you, how to select styles, and how to combine materials, you will be able to dress distinctively, in good taste, and much more economically than your neighbor who has not taken time to study the principles of dress and what it means in the way of adornment, developing ideals, and ultimate economy.

Women who know but little about sewing often marvel at the woman who at a glance can tell from the material just what style would be best suited to that material, or who, when she sees a person, can say quickly and with authority what kind of dress that person should wear to bring out her individual type of beauty.

Ability in this direction is usually attributed to cleverness or unusual talent; however, you who understand dress harmony can acquire such ability. With a thorough understanding of line, material, and color you will be able to determine instantly the fitness of certain lines to certain types, and you can broaden your knowledge by carefully observing individuals and styles and the way in which individuals adapt certain styles to themselves.

GETTING IDEAS FROM GOOD AND BAD DRESSERS

The true artist does not mar nor disfigure the surface he wishes to decorate; rather, he works with one thought in mind—beauty of the whole. The dressmaker or home woman who makes really beautiful garments must have not only the qualifications of a designer, but the artistic sense of the artist—must understand line and its relation to color and the individual

An excellent way in which you may acquire a broad, practical knowledge of good line is to observe carefully and discriminately the women who wear really nice clothes and those who wear really ordinary clothes.

Women in dowdy clothes rarely show evidence of style or thought of design, nor do they show any regard for the essentials of correct dress; thus they teach the observer to avoid any such condition in making up garments

Women who wear really good garments will serve other women as an inspiration to better dressing, and their costumes will suggest possibilities in other fabrics, colors, and designs

To achieve distinctiveness in dress, never overlook the opportunity of going where good clothes are to be seen—receptions, parties, club meetings, in fact, all places where different kinds of costumes are worn. Study the suitability of the garment for the occasion. Study closely the accessories to the costume, and note how they bring out or detract from the costume itself; then, in matters regarding your own dress or the dress of others, you will be able to suggest little touches that will enhance the beauty of a costume and add materially to its attractiveness.

The theater is an excellent field of inspiration for constructive development in good dressing, not only from the point of correct and pleasing line and color in dress, but as an expression of character or type and appropriateness of environment and occasion.

A successful actress, as I have said before, not infrequently owes a large measure of her success to a close and intelligent study of dress

Far-seeing theater managers demand a strict adherence to the best in prevailing and historical modes, knowing that, even when not fully understood by all their public, the natural feeling of pleasure and satisfaction obtained from the presentation of correct costuming has much to do with the ultimate success of their production.

It is frequently said that the church-going women folk evidence splendid taste in dress, and that the clothes they wear are excellent style criterions, because they are appropriate for the majority.

A prominent New York designer made a practice of attending a Fifth Avenue church to study the styles of the women in attendance. It may perchance seem irreverent to consider fashion in connection with church. But how many times at Sunday dinner, when the text of the sermon has been discussed, does not some member of the family say, "Did you notice what a pretty dress or hat Miss or Mrs. So and So had on this morning?"

"The artisan hurries through his work to get his dinner; the artist hurries through his dinner to get to his work," is a saying that may well be applied directly to the person who is conscientiously interested in the study of clothes.

You will study clothes and admire or criticize them according to your taste and your knowledge of what clothes express.

READY-TO-WEAR GARMENTS AS AN AID

Ready-to-wear garments are also worthy of study in developing good taste in dress.

Such garments are constructed as nearly as manufacturers can plan to please the masses of women, in the majority of cases being hurriedly made and without much regard for workmanship. Rather than durability or practicability of the garment, it is the general outline—the style effect—they strive for, and it is for this reason that the dressmaker or the woman who makes her own clothes should observe such garments carefully.

Oftentimes ready-to-wear garments display a smartness produced by the carefully careless way they are put together, a smartness that is often lost—killed, as it were—by the woman who sews too carefully and too well. It is well to remember this, and learn from ready-to-wear garments, when making clothes for yourself, to strive occasionally for effect rather than perfection in workmanship. When both qualities are attained, namely, that of being able to impart style and good workmanship to a garment, the triumph is complete.

HINTS FROM FASHION MAGAZINES

Fashion magazines are of the utmost importance to any woman who is interested in dress.

In studying any fashion magazine, consider each figure separately. If two or more materials are used in its development, strive to determine particularly why they are employed. Proper regard for such details is valuable, for it will serve to point out to you why certain materials are required for certain styles.

Strive not to be like the woman who went to a dressmaker and said, "I want a pannier skirt. I want a little puff sleeve, but I want it in soft, clinging crêpe, because I am very fond of that material. I think it is beautiful. The softness appeals to me."

Then you will not have to be informed, as this woman was, that "crêpe was designed by the manufacturer for clinging garments and is rarely adapted to the fluffy style of the pannier skirt and puff sleeves."

Of course, taffetas, organdies, and crisp batistes are suitable for such styles, and a mental picture of a pannier skirt of crêpe and another one of taffeta will show you instantly why fabrics must be designed to suit styles and styles to suit materials.

COLOR SUGGESTIONS FROM FASHION PLATES

When you have studied individual designs enough to be able to note instantly what kind of pattern is required, as well as what kind of material is best suited to the design, and can harmoniously adapt color to the lines of the garment and fabric used, you will be able to conceive pleasing results.

It is true that the fashion people cannot produce in their fashion plates an absolute likeness of the color the textile manufacturer gives us in fabrics; nor can they give an absolutely true outline of a garment as it will appear when developed in material. However, when you understand lines you will be able to get suggestions from the color plates shown in fashion magazines and elsewhere, and with this knowledge of lines you will be able to give prominence to the color that will bring out the garment to the best advantage, to use successfully the soft, silent tones or tints where only a suggestion or variation of color is desired; also, you will be able to choose a fabric that will successfully carry out the lines suggested by a fashion drawing

INTERPRETING FASHIONS

A number of excellent fashion magazines that have no pattern service are published merely to suggest style tendencies and color and fabric combinations.

If you know patterns and have studied lines, such magazines will be invaluable to you, for you can get from them ideas and suggestions that you can incorporate in your garments.

In many cases, you may apply them more successfully than the artist has done in his drawings, because you can bring out the practicability of the garment, adapt it to the material, and give the harmonious outline that suits you.

Some of the ultra fashion books contain seemingly grotesque styles, their general make-up and their silhouette appearing impossible from a practical standpoint when their development is considered in the fabric and for the human figure

The designs in these same magazines, however, are worthy of consideration, for they contain in them illusive, impractical, but artistic, even clever, ideas that may be utilized in the production of original and pleasing garments, provided you have developed a sense of originality or initiative in dress.

For example, in some of these seemingly freakish models may be found an attractive collar or a suggestion for a cuff, a finish for the waist line, or a front closing, any one of which is particularly pleasing, and if you have an eye for the fitness of style and line to fabrics and their correct color development, you can work these around in such a way as to get results that express individuality and good taste

Modifications of these seemingly freakish modes often result, too, in the creation of garments that are decidedly distinctive and original, but still of a style that is in harmony with the original.

OTHER SOURCES OF INFORMATION

If you are anxious to know the right thing regarding matters of dress, pay strict attention also to the fashion notes given in the various magazines and newspapers.

Even advertisements pertaining to garments, materials, and so on will help you in acquiring a knowledge of the kind of material suited to your lines and your type, and will bring about a successful, harmonious development of the newest and best styles

If the fashion notes or advertisements suggest some fabric or color with which you are not familiar, go to the store where they may be seen and observe them closely. Especially is this plan a good one for you to adopt in your effort to become familiar with new fabrics, especially the coloring, weight, and texture.

If a reliable store is not accessible, a letter, with a self-addressed and stamped envelope, will usually bring samples to you from a first-class merchandise house in a few days. The names given in fashion books regarding materials and colors are generally authentic, and you can, by asking for them by name, receive just the samples desired.

Right here I want to caution you about the buying of bargain materials. Nothing is a bargain that cannot be used to advantage.

In order to buy materials intelligently, it is absolutely necessary to keep pace with style tendencies. For instance, when styles are bouffant, fluffy, and airy, it means that crêpe de Chine, soft, clinging crêpes, and the like are to be avoided. At such times, merchants throughout the country who have such materials on hand do not, as a rule, wish to carry them in stock until another season, and invariably put them on sale at a great reduction in price.

If, at the time of these sales, you have occasion to use such materials for some specific purpose, you can usually pick up bargains, and it is well to do so; however, if you can afford only a few dresses and wish always to appear smart, give considerable thought to your purchases in order to make sure that the materials selected will fill your needs

If a dress is made up in a style that is in keeping with the mode of the day, but of material that is not in keeping, it will immediately be marked as a poor attempt at smartness.

In many cases, new styles call for new fabrics, and those which a person has been accustomed to using will be absolutely out of the question, no amount of effort being possible to make them assume any semblance of the prevailing mode.

With such thoughts in mind, you should think carefully before you purchase material at the bargain counter, because it is possible that you will tie up your money in material that is not up to date and will encounter no end of difficulty in trying to reproduce the new styles with it.

Any person whose allowance for clothes is limited should always endeavor to spend every dollar to the best advantage.

ACQUIRING SUCCESSFUL RESULTS

In the development and use of good taste in dress, you must always be progressive—always on the alert for new things, new color combinations, new lines, and always ready to make use of new ideas as they are given out

The manufacturer, the designer of styles, the fashion authorities, all do their best to produce new and attractive ideas in style, color, and fabric, and if you would keep abreast of the times, take the new ideas that are offered and make the most of them; apply them to your needs in a way that is practical and serviceable. And here again is the necessity for a knowledge broad and flexible enough to enable one to take the sometimes seemingly impossible and successfully develop it.

When you are about to develop a new garment and you desire inspiration from prevailing style motifs, first ascertain from what this motif is derived—whether it is from an established or basic principle of design, pure in line and true in its relation to the lines of the figure, or whether it is a whimsical or erratic striving for something new and different in design without proper regard for its purpose, which is, or should be, that of clothing the human form comfortably and artistically. If the design cannot measure up to such points, there is no reason for its acceptance

Next, determine the time and intensity of the present vogue of the style motif; that is, the period of its first appearance and the interest or popularity it has developed or is enjoying. For example, indications of the style motif come slowly, notwithstanding many opinions to the contrary. If you believe that style changes are effected overnight, you lack a proper knowledge of what constitutes style. You are confusing style with fashion

Style is the motif, the treatment, the design, the entire ensemble, as it were, of the garment, which includes design, material, color, and workmanship; *fashion* is the popularity of a certain style, the common trend, the rage, as it may be called, the last term it would seem being fit when certain periods of women's dress are reflected on

If you desire style rather than fashion, examine the newest silhouette or outline For example, if wide, flaring skirts, natural waistline effects, and full sleeves are at the height of popular favor, search until you find a changing tendency, which will invariably be a decrease in skirt widths, the moving of the waist line, and a changing of sleeve outlines. If, on the other hand, the narrow skirt and general appearance of slimness is the silhouette preeminent, you may rest assured that a change in the other direction is inevitable.

Fashion moves like a pendulum, and you will never be dressed in faulty style or entirely out of fashion if you anticipate, after a correct analysis of current modes, what will most surely follow.

It is to your advantage, then, not only to keep up with the prevailing fashions, but to keep as far as possible abreast of the popular mode. By this study of style and fashion, along with the proper knowledge and appreciation of your needs, it is not unreasonable to assert that you may always be dressed in good style and in fashion, for the life of every garment chosen will be materially prolonged and greater satisfaction and comfort, as well as practical economy, will most surely result.

Learn to buy materials that are good, practical, durable, and beautiful; avoid eccentricities, and choose lines that are in accord with your type of figure Then your gown or suit will be agreeably appropriate for two years rather than for six months.

To be constantly awake to new things does not mean that everything must be adopted; it means that through your thorough knowledge of lines, color, and fabrics, you will be able to discard the bad and choose only the things that will give satisfactory results and be pleasing and serviceable

To know dress well is to keep growing. You cannot afford to feel satisfied that you know all there is to be known about clothes. You must remember that many persons are devoting hours of earnest effort each day in bringing out the very best things in fabrics, style, and color, and that these people, as they are experts in their lines, can give you many good ideas and help you achieve your desires by aiding you in keeping you informed on the ever-changing problems of dress.

Always work for a happy medium, and never allow yourself to get into a rut regarding your clothes. It is well to keep style and color constantly in mind, never losing sight of yourself, for few are ideal in either face or figure and frequently require modified styles to bring out their charm or individual beauty.

Individual development of style is one thing that makes the clever individual's interpretation superior to ready-to-wear garments, and when consideration is given to the durability or lasting qualities of a garment that is carefully made by one who understands dress, such garments are so much superior to ready-to-wear garments that there is no comparison.

Regard dress and its correct use and development as an art, just as the musician or the painter considers his work an art. Strive to have your dresses creations—harmonious pictures.

Such dresses may be created by a combination of certain factors that produce a oneness of effect, a harmoniously pleasing result; and as you develop a garment you will be satisfied or dissatisfied with the result according to the ideal you have set for your work and to the amount of thought and effort that you have put into it.

There is always great opportunity for the woman who is willing to give plenty of study and earnest effort and thought to the designing and making of her clothes.

Many of our greatest creators of fashion in an effort to get a desired effect labor over a certain gown or suit for seemingly unreasonable lengths of time. Surrounded by yards of chiffon, silks, laces, and similar materials from which they can get inspiration, their every thought, in fact, their whole being, centers upon the creation in mind, and they gradually develop the thought, the effect they want, and with this done the details, the general construction, and the finishing of the garment itself seem of minor importance.

Beautiful dresses, those which stand out most prominently in fashion's history, are developed by the bringing together of certain fabrics and certain colors; and, in striving to get harmony out of their combinations, there are developed suitable lines that in many instances make striking creations.

Such effects are often produced during the development of a gown—nothing cut and dried about it; all inspired work is work of love, and in the creating of clothes, the inspiration must be supplemented by a knowledge of color combinations, fabric combinations, and lines

Such garments are, as a rule, creations in every sense of the word—a work of art—for they are generally artistic and harmonious There is life to such garments. They are usually strong in line and show evidence of development by a master hand. Only by such devotion, by a full appreciation of all the elements of garment construction, and a continual striving for the beautiful, are these creations possible.

The woman making dresses for herself must have studied dress principles enough to support her own ideals

From what has been said you will readily see that the development of good taste in line, color, material, and suitability as to color combination of material and to style of the garment are arrived at only by diligent study of the artistic and practical relation of one to the other; then application and the determination to apply them to yourself are the mediums through which excellent results are expressed. Sustained work, conscientious study, and a pride in achievement will bring forth results that spasmodic effort never can.

You may not always be satisfied with your result, no matter if you have put a great amount of labor, conscientious thought, and honest effort into the production of a garment. When it is completed you will see where certain things that would improve it might have gone into the gown. Strive to have each new garment an improvement on the last by incorporating in it the good points missing in the one before.

And as you go on and develop clothes for yourself, and, as I have suggested, dress up your friends by planning in your mind what they should wear and why they should wear certain things, you will acquire not only the correct principles of dress, but the high ideals of dress—ideals that will put dress and its mission in the high position it should have in your mind.

Your consideration about dress, your correct adherence to the principles and the carrying out of your ideals, will make your friends and acquaintances take notice of you and will invariably awaken in them a desire for the right kind of clothes.

So, you see, it is an endless chain, for if you will lay the foundation for the understanding of dress, as in any other subject, you will have a following and an opportunity to do much toward helping American women to be distinctively clothed.

YOUR STYLE

Your style is important. Ask yourself every time you buy anything, every time you make anything, or have anything made: Is it in accord with *my* style? Does it meet the requirements of correct dress for *me?*

If you live in a little city or a village and suddenly find yourself on Fifth Avenue in New York City, would you feel conspicuous in your clothes? If you had friends from the fashion centers of America coming to visit you, would you feel out of place in your costume? You should not. You have the same opportunity to be correctly dressed as any other woman if you will study and persevere toward perfection in dress

We must realize that we have a style of our own and that we are of a particular type. This is recognized by every fashion authority in the country, and by every fashion publication, for if all women were to adhere to one fashion, one fashion only would be shown in the fashion books instead of twenty, thirty, or fifty different designs.

Look through any fashion book today and you will find round-and-round and up-and-down lines in the same issue—all with the idea of helping women to clothe themselves correctly and of giving suggestions that will help them individually to find appropriate styles

Establishing a style for yourself and then perfecting it—be it in hats, gloves, shoes, dresses, or suits—will prove economical, and it will not be long before a degree of perfection will be acquired

A prominent New York business woman, who is one of the most distinctively dressed women that I know, wears the smartest suits and hats and always severely tailor-made gowns. And her neckwear, usually a jabot or a stock, is so smart that you would never for a minute question but what it is authoritatively fashionable. She always wears high shoes on the street, and usually they have light-colored tops, because she is tall and the light tops of the shoes help to break the appearance of height.

One day, this young woman came to visit me. I could not refrain from remarking about the completeness of her costume. I said, "If I saw your shadow, I should know that it was you by the harmony that your silhouette expresses and the very way you carry yourself."

She said, "Do you know that remarks like yours is what caused me to persevere in acquiring my style of dressing? I used to think I wanted loose, floppy clothes in which I could relax and be just as free and comfortable as if I were in negligée Once, when in a ferry boat crossing New York harbor, I saw sitting opposite me a line of crumpled-up women apparently enjoying their slovenly posture. Not one of them expressed dignity or pride in her personal appearance. Not one of the women on that boat, I thought, was unusual or had any desire to know better. I then took a little self-inventory I was ashamed of myself, because I realized that I was not very much better dressed than other women on the boat. I sat up straight and determined right then and there that I would acquire a style becoming and practical for me and would express that style in the most attractive and agreeable way that I could. And that resolution has helped me more than I can say."

She was frank enough to tell me that she attributed a great part of her success to having wakened up, to having made herself trim and having kept herself so. She always plans to have one good suit or one good dress—just as good as she possibly can afford; she procures a garment that she has to respect, and that will make her "dress up to fit."

She said, "If I put on a shabby dress, I will allow my shoes to be shabby and will be careless about my personal grooming; but when I have a dress that I have to be particular about, I always have my hair, my shoes, my gloves, my corset—everything—just right for it, and I always look very much better."

Living up to your clothes, creating a style, and being equal to an intelligent expression of it, is worth many dollars to a woman who wants to be a success in business, in the home, or in social life

CHAPTER IX

ECONOMY IN DRESS

ECONOMY WITHOUT CHEAPNESS—CLOTHES CONSERVATION—CLOTHES-CLOSET EXPLOITS—A PLEDGE FOR AMERICAN WOMEN.

History, when it gives us a peep into the interesting intimacies of our foremothers and chats with us in a friendly way about their dress, never seems to deem flamboyant or moneyed dress worthy of emphasis in historic chronicling.

Read in the fashion notes of past centuries and you will find that simple dress, which is almost invariably artistic dress, was held in favor by those who knew and that it always lived longest.

The dignified and unpretentious Puritan costume will ever be cherished and modeled after, because it fitted in and was right for the spirit and purse of the women who wore it.

Flamboyant dress is rank extravagance—wilful waste. Cheap dress, too, is extravagance, because it soon loses its livability and must be replaced sooner than would a dress of good material, design, and workmanship.

I have never had patience with a woman who spends all the money she can on her clothes, who considers it "poor folksy" to make over clothes. Rather, I like to use my knowledge of clothes values to dress economically and yet attain success in dress; and, most of all, I like to do this in make-over clothes. I find actual pleasure in showing respect to fabrics and pieces of trimming that have served me well by adapting them to a new fashion with the greatest skill I possess.

In "Thrift," by Smiles, we may read this adequate definition: "Economy is . . . the growth of experience, example, and forethought. It is only when men become wise and thoughtful that they become frugal."

To practice economy in dress without cheapness, it is necessary to apply the principles of dress to the requirements of your individual type. Throughout this book, paragraphs upon paragraphs are given on the principles of dress, the triangle of correct dress that surrounds the individual—i. e., color, line, and fabric. A knowledge of these three things correctly applied will bring about economy in dress. You will be able to dress in better taste and at far less expense when you understand the principles and adhere to them with a will for success.

A wise and fair expenditure of income is one of the greatest economical factors of the age and one of the most vital of the household problems. The woman who is in charge of the household purse has a responsibility as great as that of earning to fill it, if not greater, and it is her duty to inform herself as to the cost and the return on every purchase she makes if she would spend wisely and well.

Much has been written on clothes budgets. Personally, I have never been able to apply a clothes-budget outline to my needs. Sometimes a certain dress is so much of a success that I can wear it two or three years. Other times, perhaps the next season, I want to make over the dress that I seem to have outgrown mentally rather than physically. Then, again, I find that something new—a new frock, a new hat, or a new veil—is a wise investment, in that the purchase and wear give me happiness, and that is as I wish it to be. I like to enjoy planning, purchasing, and wearing clothes. I revel in a trifling purchase if it is something to harmonize with something else I own or to fill a definite need.

If you plan every little detail of your costume with regard to your type and individuality, you will find that you will wear this costume twice as long as if you bought it through necessity or without anticipating the joy of ownership.

CLOTHES CONSERVATION

The most economically dressed business woman I know is one of the smartest dressed women I know. She actually practices clothes conservation Her clothes seem so much a part of her that everything she wears seems to have a definite place and to fill it well

I know this woman intimately, and know, too, that she wore one extremely well-tailored blue-serge frock to business for two years. She also has one blue-silk dress, which she wore to afternoon and evening affairs. During this time, her extravagances, if they could be called that, were dainty new collars and cuffs. Usually, these were made and carefully laundered by her own hands. It seemed that a dainty, "just-right" collar always completed her toilet, and I am sure that if you were to see this woman, no matter where, you would say she was smartly gowned. True, she had a beautiful fur piece and a handsome coat, but both of these she had had longer than two years. You could never associate "out-of-dateness" with anything she wore, because her garments were as simple as it is possible to have them, and she kept them immaculate. I have heard her say that if she even senses a weak spot in one of her precious frocks she darns it immediately.

She says now: "I never enjoyed my clothes more, and I shall never own more than four dresses at a time as long as I live. I derive actual pleasure in making my very self a standard regarding my clothes and living up to that standard, for I find more joy that way and it is ever so much more comfortable and a great deal more economical."

This woman makes her own dresses, insisting that this gives her great advantages, because she can purchase excellent material and economize in cutting; and then she is sure that the garments will be exactly suited to her individual requirements. This she deems the most important factor in successful dress. She says she found it easier to learn to make her clothes successfully than it was to try to have her desires interpreted by a dressmaker or satisfied by ready-to-wear garments.

Respect for fabrics and deep appreciation of hand work, a carefully supplied mending basket, an acquaintance, too, with the iron and its smooth career, together with a few handy recipes for removing spots and stains, will help any woman to practice fair economy—an economy she will enjoy, for there is an element of thrift and personal pride that one feels in such work. Even the menial, yet necessary, task of shining one's shoes has its virtues, for one never undertakes such a task without becoming eager to do more in the way of freshening up.

CLOTHES-CLOSET EXPLOITS

I have always said that if I were an architect I would plan the closets first and then the house around them in order to have ample closet room. But, with all the importance I give to clothes closets, I must admit that there are times when they actually encourage extravagance.

They do it in this way: We think we haven't anything to wear. We need new shoes or a new wrap, forgetting that we have in the closets available material that could be freshened up. If it is a dress, perhaps it could be made over to some extent, or, if necessary, entirely remodeled.

Every once in a while you will find it economical to make an exploit through your clothes closet Then, when you have made a careful inventory, see whether your conscience will permit you to buy new clothes or not. Usually one's conscience is a good criterion to follow after a clothes-closet exploit.

A PLEDGE FOR AMERICAN WOMEN

If I could send out a pledge card to American women regarding dress, I would make the pledge read thus:

As an American woman, I pledge myself to strive always to acquire and wear only such clothes as are appropriate and individually becoming; to avoid extremes in design and color, to respect my clothes enough to care for them to the best of my ability; and to select my clothes so that, in fairness to them, they may give back to me in service more than they cost me in money. I further pledge myself to help establish for all time, by regularly applying the rules of correct dress to myself, the fact that American women are the best dressed women in the entire land.

OLGA PETROVA

An erect figure with distinctive carriage, a woman who wears simple or elaborate clothes with distinctiveness

Copyright, Marceau

CHAPTER X

DISTINCTIVE DRESS

PERSONALITY AND MENTALITY—AN INTERESTING PERSONALITY—THE A B C OF DISTINCTIVE DRESS

In the beginning of this book, I told you—but not in so many words—that mentality is as great a factor in being an attractive woman as is dress. If you have come with me all the way through the book, and understand what I have endeavored to convey to you, you will be fully convinced of this.

Just suppose we are at a dinner party. A beautiful woman dressed in perfect taste sits near us. We attempt conversation with her, but she does not know how to respond and we lose our interest in her. We were fascinated by a beautiful picture that will not bear close acquaintance, because her mentality is not equal to her physical beauty.

We immediately wonder how it is that she is beautifully gowned and whether her gown was designed and constructed according to her own ideas, or according to those of some person whose intelligence is greater than hers.

On the other hand, what a joy it is to see a correctly dressed woman who possesses personality and mentality. When we open conversation with her, we find that her mentality fairly scintillates; her thoughts are ever quick and ready, her ideals high and inspiring, and her sympathy broad and generous.

Mentality is so much a part of attractiveness that no woman who is earnest in her desire to be appropriately dressed can afford to be lackadaisical in matters that pertain to her intellectual equipment.

AN INTERESTING PERSONALITY

Some one may say: "I believe I could reach the heights of correct dress. I have an attractive face and a pleasing figure, but I am not interesting."

I want to say to you earnestly, an interesting personality may be acquired, and quickly, too, if one is interested and desirous of acquiring human understanding—of acquiring love for the humanness expressed all around us Reading, observation, association, all help to form a generous mind, and sympathetic human interest in everything that concerns us and those about us will help to develop the generous mind and make it possible for its owner to be both charming and interesting.

Learn to enjoy your surroundings, to appreciate your associates. None are so ill-disposed that you cannot find hidden away somewhere, if you know how to bring them out, a responsive chord and frequently much lovableness.

And the same is true of work, no matter what it is; good is somewhere about if we look for it. No work is so common that it cannot help us if our own minds are receptive and open to improvement.

In dress this is perhaps more noticeably true than in anything else. I have seen women develop their ideas of dress to a delightful degree in just a few short weeks, because they allowed their minds to be open to improvement. They saw the need of being better dressed; they were awakened to the fact that they could be more attractive, that they could give happiness to others and acquire a keener self-respect by cultivating good taste in dress. When minds are awake to dress possibilities, they will also be awake to other things of interest, thereby aiding them to develop interesting personalities.

Many people ask, "Why do actresses apparently express more intelligence in dress than does the average woman?"

The answer is simple. It is because an actress to be successful in her art must first of all develop her mind by long and diligent study, and, second, she must use her grace of body and her clothes to express to perfection the part she plays.

The reason, then, that a successful actress invariably expresses her personality in her dress must be attributed to the fact that she studies and strives for certain effects, and, through study and her intense earnestness, achieves her goal.

Knowledge of the correct principles of dress and a close adherence to them will aid you in acquiring personal assurance, which is the keynote of success.

Personal assurance is gained by a thorough understanding of the undertaking we have in hand—be it work, play, or what you will—and being entirely fit mentally and physically to meet the demands that are made upon us.

Your physical self cannot win for you unless your state of mind, as well as your body, is comfortable.

This means that proper clothing is a big factor in your success, for mentality acts behind the mask of body, and the body must be equal to express it. You must back up your mentality, emphasize your personality, acquire personal assurance by knowing that your clothes are absolutely right.

Support the "within" by correctly attiring the "without," and half your battle is won for you.

THE A B C OF DISTINCTIVE DRESS

In summing up, the A B C of distinctive dress is *careful grooming* and *correct attire.*

If your attire is entirely correct, it will always be appropriate. Vigilance must be exercised in carrying out the minute details of grooming as well as costume. Begin today to "take care of yourself"—your mental as well as physical self—and in a surprisingly short time you will have achieved your goal—you will have acquired the charm of mind and of manner and the self-reliance that comes to those who know the "Secrets of Distinctive Dress."

Lightning Source UK Ltd.
Milton Keynes UK
UKHW020634071222
413510UK00004B/39

9 780343 312732